MY REVISION NOTES

OCR

GCSE (9–1)

COMPUTER SCIENCE

3RD EDITION

George Rouse

Boost

HODDER
EDUCATION
AN HACHETTE UK COMPANY

This book draws on material written for and published in OCR GCSE Computer Science, Second Edition (978 1 5104 8416 0) by George Rouse, Lorne Pearcey and Gavin Craddock. The publisher would like to thank Lorne Pearcey and Gavin Craddock for permission to re-use their work in the present volume.

Lorne Pearcey and Gavin Craddock have not written any content specifically for this revision guide, including the exam-style questions and examiner's tips.

The Publishers would like to thank the following for permission to reproduce copyright material.

Photo credits
Figure 1.5.1: Background photograph © Mike Berenson/Colorado Captures/Getty Images

Acknowledgements
Adobe is either a registered trademark or trademark of Adobe in the United States and/or other countries.

Google and the Google logo are registered trademarks of Google LLC, used with permission.

Microsoft product screenshot(s) used with permission from Microsoft.

Microsoft and Windows are either registered trademarks or trademarks of Microsoft Corporation in the United States and/or other countries.

Every effort has been made to trace all copyright holders, but if any have been inadvertently overlooked, the Publishers will be pleased to make the necessary arrangements at the first opportunity.

Although every effort has been made to ensure that website addresses are correct at time of going to press, Hodder Education cannot be held responsible for the content of any website mentioned in this book. It is sometimes possible to find a relocated web page by typing in the address of the home page for a website in the URL window of your browser.

Hachette UK's policy is to use papers that are natural, renewable and recyclable products and made from wood grown in well-managed forests and other controlled sources. The logging and manufacturing processes are expected to conform to the environmental regulations of the country of origin.

Orders: please contact Hachette UK Distribution, Hely Hutchinson Centre, Milton Road, Didcot, Oxfordshire, OX11 7HH. Telephone: +44 (0)1235 827827. Email education@hachette.co.uk Lines are open from 9 a.m. to 5 p.m., Monday to Friday. You can also order through our website: www.hoddereducation.co.uk

ISBN: 978 1 3983 2114 4

First published in 2021 by
Hodder Education,
An Hachette UK Company
Carmelite House
50 Victoria Embankment
London EC4Y 0DZ

www.hoddereducation.co.uk

Impression number   10 9 8 7 6 5 4 3 2

Year   2025 2024 2023

Cover photo © Patrick P. Palej - stock.adobe.com

Illustrations by Aptara, Inc. and Integra Software Services Pvt. Ltd

Typeset in India by Aptara, Inc.

Printed and bound by CPI Group (UK) Ltd, Croydon, CR0 4YY

A catalogue record for this title is available from the British Library.

Get the most from this book

Everyone has to decide his or her own revision strategy, but it is essential to learn your work, review it and test your understanding. These Revision Notes will help you to do that in a planned way, topic by topic. Use this book as the cornerstone of your revision and don't hesitate to write in it – personalise your notes and check your progress by ticking off each section as you revise.

Tick to track your progress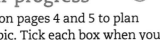

Use the revision planner on pages 4 and 5 to plan your revision, topic by topic. Tick each box when you have:

+ revised and understood a topic
+ tested yourself
+ practised the exam questions and gone online to check your answers.

You can also keep track of your revision by ticking off each topic heading in the book. You may find it helpful to add your own notes as you work through each topic.

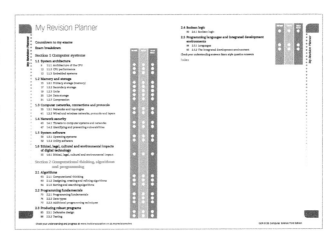

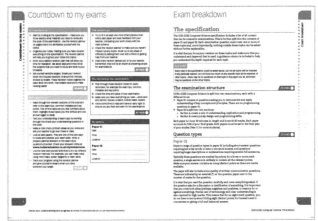

Features to help you succeed

Exam tip

Expert tips to help polish your exam technique and maximise your chances in the exam

Common mistake

Common mistakes that candidates make and how to avoid them.

Check your understanding

Questions to test your understanding of basic facts.

Worked example

Worked examples illustrate methods, calculations and explanations.

Now test yourself

Activities to encourage note taking and revision.

Key point

Further explanation of some important issues.

Exam-style questions

Practice exam questions to consolidate your revision and practise your exam skills.

Definitions of **key terms** that need additional explanation are provided where they first appear.

My Revision Planner

2.4 Boolean logic

2.5 Programming languages and integrated development environments

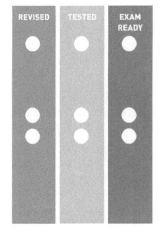

My Revision Planner

Countdown to my exams

6–8 weeks to go

- Start by looking at the specification – make sure you know exactly what material you need to revise and the style of the examination. Use the revision planner on pages 4 and 5 to familiarise yourself with the topics.
- Organise your notes, making sure you have covered everything on the specification. The revision planner will help you to group your notes into topics.
- Work out a realistic revision plan that will allow you time for relaxation. Set aside days and times for all the subjects that you need to study and stick to your timetable.
- Set yourself sensible targets. Break your revision down into focused sessions of around 40 minutes, divided by breaks. These Revision Notes organise the basic facts into short, memorable sections to make revising easier.

REVISED

2–6 weeks to go

- Read through the relevant sections of this book and refer to the exam tips, common mistakes and key points. Tick off the topics as you feel confident about them. Highlight those topics you find difficult and look at them again in detail.
- Test your understanding of each topic by working through the Check your understanding questions in the book.
- Make a note of any problem areas as you revise and ask your teacher to go over these in class.
- Look at past papers. They are one of the best ways to revise and practise your exam skills. Write or prepare planned answers to the exam-style questions provided. Check your answers.
- Use the Now test yourself activities to try out different revision methods. For example, you can make notes using mind maps, spider diagrams or flash cards.
- Track your progress using the revision planner and give yourself a reward when you have achieved your target.

REVISED

One week to go

- Try to fit in at least one more timed practice of an entire past paper and seek feedback from your teacher, comparing your work closely with the mark scheme.
- Check the revision planner to make sure you haven't missed out any topics. Brush up on any areas of difficulty by talking them over with a friend or getting help from your teacher.
- Attend any revision classes put on by your teacher. Remember, they will be an expert at preparing people for examinations.

REVISED

The day before the examination

- Browse through these Revision Notes for useful reminders, for example the exam tips, common mistakes and key points.
- Check the time and place of your examination.
- Make sure you have everything you need – extra pens and pencils, tissues, a watch, bottled water, sweets.
- Allow some time to relax and have an early night to ensure you are fresh and alert for the examinations.

REVISED

My exams

Paper 01

Date: ....

Time: ....

Location: ....

Paper 02

Date: ....

Time: ....

Location: ....

Exam breakdown

The specification

The OCR GCSE Computer Science specification includes a list of all content that can be covered in examinations. This is further split into the contents of paper 01 and paper 02. Each examination question must cover one or more of these topics and, more importantly, nothing outside these topics can be asked without further explanation.

It is vital that you focus your revision on these topics and make sure that you understand each keyword that is used. A guidance column is included to help you understand the depth required for each topic.

> **Key point**
>
> Every topic in the specification could be asked about, but not all topics will be included in any particular session. Do not focus too much on any specific topic at the expense of other topics – there may be no questions on that topic in the paper you sit, and there may be questions on the other topics.

The examination structure

OCR's GCSE Computer Science is split into two examinations, each with a different focus:

+ Paper 01 consists of questions asking you to demonstrate and apply understanding of key concepts and principles. There are no programming questions in paper 01.
+ Paper 02 is split into two sections:
    + Section A covers a mix of understanding, application and programming.
    + Section B covers purely design and programming skills.

Each paper is 1 hour 30 minutes in length and is worth 80 marks. Each paper accounts for 50% of your final grade. Both papers must be sat in the final year of your studies (Year 11 for most students).

Question types

Paper 01

Expect a range of question types in paper 01 including short answer questions requiring just a few words or even a one-word answer, and questions requiring longer descriptions or explanations requiring several full sentences.

Typically these questions are marked by points; for a three or more mark question, a single sentence is unlikely to contain all the relevant points. Make sure your answer contains as many distinct points as there are marks available.

The paper will also include some quality of written communication questions. These are indicated by an asterisk (*) on the question paper next to the number of marks for the question.

It is vital that you read the question carefully and cover everything asked. If the question asks for a discussion or justification of something, it is important that you cover both sides (perhaps negatives and positives, or reasons for or against something). Precise use of terminology and clear understanding is also required for high marks. This means that for an eight-mark question, you do not have to worry about hitting eight distinct points but instead need to concentrate on giving a full and balanced answer.

Paper 02

Paper 02 contains questions that ask you to design, write and refine algorithms. The approach for these differs between the two sections of the paper.

In Section A, pseudocode, high-level English sentences and flowcharts would be acceptable methods of answering. Equally, OCR Reference Language or a suitable high-level language could be used. In Section A, you are assessed on understanding the steps that need to be taken.

In Section B, answers must be given using OCR Reference Language or a suitable high-level language. Minor syntax errors will not be penalised, but the examiner must be able to see that you would be able to get the required solution working on a computer.

For all algorithm questions, there may be many possible answers. Examiners will trace through your answer and check whether it would work logically. If a solution would work, it should achieve high marks.

If a question asks you to design a solution, this will generally involve some form of structure diagram or a flowchart. The important element is to show the steps that need to be taken to solve the problem; there is no need to use a high-level language for this. The answer to a question using the command word 'write' will require a high-level language or OCR Reference Language to be used. For this, it is best to imagine that you are writing the program on a computer in your preferred language.

Testing a solution involves taking an existing program and checking that it works properly. This can be done by using a test plan (which may or may not be provided for you in the question) alongside suitable test data.

A question using the command word 'refine' is asking you to improve whatever is given to you. It could be that the program does not work and so, after discovering what doesn't work through testing, you would be expected to write a version that does actually work.

Alternatively, you may be given some code that is inefficient in some way and be expected to write a version that completes the same task in a shorter number of steps.

In exam questions for both papers, questions using programming language will present the programming code using OCR Reference Language. You will be able to use this language in your answers. You can find details and examples of how it will be used on the OCR website:

ocr.org.uk

(search for J277 programming language to find the relevant information).

1.1 System architecture

A computer system consists of hardware and software working together to process data.

Hardware is the name for the physical components that make up the computer system.

Software is the name for the programs that provide instructions for the computer, telling it what to do.

A computer system receives information as an input, processes and stores that information, and then outputs the results of that processing.

The CPU processes the data.

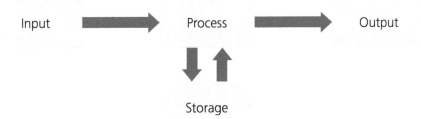

Figure 1.1.1 Input–process–output

1.1.1 Architecture of the CPU

Purpose of the CPU

The purpose of the CPU is to carry out a set of instructions that is contained in a computer program.

It does this using the fetch–execute cycle.
+ Fetch – an instruction in the form of data is retrieved from main memory.
+ Decode – the CPU decodes the instruction.
+ Execute – the CPU performs an action according to the instruction.

The CPU operates at high speeds governed by the clock chip.
+ The clock chip uses a vibrating crystal to maintain a constant speed.
+ The speed of the clock chip is measured in hertz, Hz (cycles per second) and typically works at up to 4 GHz (four billion cycles per second).
+ The clock speed is the number of fetch–execute cycles per second.

> The CPU is a collection of billions of electronic switches that process data, execute instructions and control the operation of the computer.
>
> The fetch–execute cycle is the basic operation of the CPU. It continually fetches, decodes and executes instructions stored in memory.

Common CPU components and their function

Arithmetic Logic Unit (ALU)

The ALU carries out the calculations and logical decisions required by the program instructions that the CPU is processing.
+ Arithmetic operations, such as add and subtract.
+ Logical operations, such as AND, OR and NOT, and the result of 'less than', 'greater than', 'equal to' comparisons.
+ Binary shift operations, which are used for multiplication or division.

Control unit (CU)

The CU co-ordinates the activity of the CPU and memory in order to execute instructions. It:
+ sends out signals to control how data moves around the CPU and memory
+ decodes instructions from memory.

Cache memory

The purpose of cache memory is to provide temporary storage that the CPU can access very quickly.
+ It stores instructions and data that are used repeatedly or are likely to be required for the next CPU operation.

Cache memory sits between the processor and main memory (RAM).
+ The CPU looks in the cache for required data.
+ If it is not there, it requests it from RAM.
+ The data is moved into cache before being accessed by the CPU.

Registers

In Von Neumann architecture, data and instructions are stored in the same memory.

Typical Von Neumann architecture uses a number of registers.

Registers are memory locations within the CPU that hold data temporarily and can be accessed very quickly.

Their role in the CPU is to accept, store and transfer data and instructions for immediate use by the CPU.

Four of the registers found in the CPU are the ACC, PC, MDR and MAR.

Accumulator (ACC)
+ Stores the results of any calculations made by the Arithmetic Logic Unit (ALU).
+ Stores the value of inputs and outputs to and from the CPU.

Program counter (PC)
+ Keeps track of the memory location (known as an address) for the next instruction.
+ The program counter is incremented (increased by 1) to the next memory location at the fetch stage of the fetch–execute cycle, to allow the program to be executed line by line.
+ Program instructions can modify the value in the program counter to alter the flow of the program so that it continues from a new location.

Memory data register (MDR)
+ Stores any data fetched from memory or any data that is to be transferred to and stored in memory.

Memory address register (MAR)
+ Stores the location in memory (an address) to be used by the MDR – that is, where the MDR needs to fetch data from or send data to.

Note: You do not need to know about buses for your examination.

Figure 1.1.2 is a simplified diagram showing the layout of these components, and how the CPU communicates with memory and input/output devices.

Von Neumann architecture is the most common organisation of computer components, where instructions and data are stored in the same place.

Exam tip

Questions on these topics often require you to know these definitions.

Exam tip

You will often be asked about what type of information is held in each of these registers, an address or data or an instruction. Just saying data or address is not enough, you must explain more about the data or address.

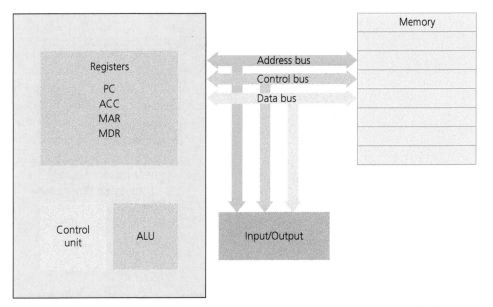

Figure 1.1.2 A CPU with Von Neumann architecture; the arrows represent the flow of data between components

The fetch–execute cycle in more detail

Fetch

1   Each instruction in a computer program is stored in a particular location (or address) in memory. The address of the next instruction is copied from the program counter and placed in the MAR.
2   The MAR now contains a memory address. The control unit fetches the data that is stored at that address and copies it to the MDR.
3   The program counter is incremented to point to the next instruction to be processed in the program, ready for the next fetch–execute cycle.

Decode

4   The MDR now contains either data to be processed by the CPU, fetched from memory, or an instruction. The control unit decodes the instruction to see what to do.

Execute

5   The decoded instruction is executed. This might mean performing a calculation using the ALU, locating some data in memory, changing the program counter value – or something else.

Once the execute part of the cycle is complete, the next fetch–execute cycle begins.

Revision activity

Load a web version of Little Man Computer (https://peterhigginson.co.uk/lmc/) and, from the box marked 'select', choose 'add'. This will load a simple program. Run this by selecting 'step' to see how the fetch–execute process uses the key registers in the CPU to add together two numbers input by the user.

Check your understanding

1   What is the purpose of the CPU?
2   What are the **three** main stages in the fetch–execute process?
3   Identify **three** registers and what type of data they hold during the fetch–execute cycle.
4   State the key feature of Von Neumann architecture.

Answers on p. 98

1.1.2 CPU performance

How common characteristics of CPUs affect their performance

REVISED

Clock speed

The CPU is constantly fetching and executing instructions.

The speed at which it does this is determined by an electronic clock.

The faster the clock speed, the more instructions that can be executed every second.

The clock speed is measured in Hertz; 1 Hz = once per second.

Amount of cache memory

Cache memory is located between the main memory and the CPU.

It is used to hold data that needs to be accessed very quickly.

Accessing cache memory is much faster than accessing main memory.

The larger the cache memory, the more likely it is that the required data will have been copied from main memory.

The more cache memory available, the better the performance of the computer.

Number of processor cores

In a multi-core CPU there are a number of processor cores each capable of carrying out the fetch–execute cycle.

If the program supports multi-cores, the CPU can handle several instructions at the same time.

> **Exam tip**
>
> You need to know how all of these factors work together to determine how quickly the computer works.

> **Key point**
>
> Cache memory is significantly more expensive than main memory (RAM) and a typical computer will only have KB of cache compared to GB of RAM.

> **Exam tip**
>
> Having multiple cores does not necessarily improve the performance of the computer. This only works if the program has been developed to use multiple cores and the program running is capable of being split into subsections.

> **Check your understanding**
>
> 5 Describe the **three** factors that affect the performance of the computer.
>
> **Answers on p. 98**

1.1.3 Embedded systems

The purpose and characteristics of embedded systems

REVISED

An **embedded system** is a computer system that has a dedicated function as part of a larger device.

When a computer device is required to perform a single or fixed range of tasks, it can be engineered to reduce its size and complexity in order to focus only on these tasks.

Dedicated software will be programmed into the device to complete the necessary tasks and nothing else.

The reduction of complexity of the hardware and the dedicated nature of the software will make the device more reliable and cost-effective than using a general-purpose computer.

The main components of a computer are either manufactured onto a single chip (a microcontroller), or separate circuits for processing and memory are combined into a larger device.

The embedded system will typically include some ROM (read-only memory) to store the dedicated program and some RAM to store user inputs and processor outputs.

Embedded systems have the following characteristics.
+ **Low power** so they can operate effectively from a small power source such as in a mobile phone.
+ **Small size** so they can fit into portable devices such as a personal fitness device.
+ **Rugged** so that they can operate in harsh environments such as car engine management systems or in military applications.
+ **Low cost** so that they are suitable for use in mass-produced, low-cost devices such as microwave ovens.
+ **Dedicated software** to complete a single task or limited range of tasks, such as in computer aided manufacture or control systems.

Examples of embedded systems

Embedded systems are found within common household devices such as:
+ washing machines
+ set-top boxes
+ telephones
+ televisions
+ home security and control systems.

Embedded systems are also widely used within larger and more complex systems, such as:
+ car engine management
+ airplane avionics
+ computer-controlled manufacturing
+ military applications such as guidance systems.

Embedded systems are frequently connected to the internet via Wi-Fi to exchange data with third parties or apps on other devices, such as:
+ water meters
+ energy smart meters
+ home security
+ central heating management systems.

> **Exam tip**
>
> It is useful to think about what data is input and output by common devices with embedded systems and what is held in ROM and RAM. Think also about the environment in which the device operates to identify which features of the embedded system make them appropriate.

Examples of embedded system inputs and outputs:

System	Input examples	Output examples
washing machine	choice of program	display progress
	water temperature	signal to heater
	water level	signal to water input valve
satnav	destination	driving instructions
	GPS position	current location mapped

> **Check your understanding**
>
> 6 Describe **three** features that make an embedded system appropriate for use in a small drone helicopter.
>
> **Answers on p. 98**

Exam checklist

In this chapter you learned about:

The purpose of the CPU
+ To carry out a set of instructions contained in a computer program using the fetch–execute cycle

Common CPU components and their function
+ ALU to carry out arithmetic calculations and logical decisions
+ CU to decode instructions and control how data moves in the CPU to execute the instructions
+ Cache memory to temporarily hold instructions and data that the CPU is likely to need
+ Registers, which are memory locations within the CPU that hold data

Von Neumann architecture
+ In Von Neumann architecture, data and instructions are stored in the same memory
+ Four key registers in Von Neumann architecture are:
    + Accumulator to store the results of calculations carried out by the ALU
    + Program counter to hold the address of the next instruction
    + Memory data register to hold the data fetched from memory or to be sent to memory
    + Memory address register to hold the address of the next memory location to be accessed

How common characteristics of CPUs affect their performance
+ Clock speed
+ Cache memory
+ Number of cores

The purpose and characteristics of embedded systems
+ Designed for a dedicated function as part of a bigger system
+ Often manufactured as a single chip
+ Dedicated hardware and software to perform a limited set of tasks
+ Programs often uploaded at manufacturing stage
+ Limited options to modify the programs
+ Low power consumption
+ Small
+ Rugged
+ Low cost

Now test yourself

TESTED ○

1 Make a list of the main components of the CPU and what they do.
2 List the stages of the fetch–execute cycle and what happens at each stage.
3 Make a list of the factors that affect the speed of the CPU.
4 List some embedded systems and identify the inputs and outputs.

Exam-style questions

1 A computer is advertised as having a clock speed of 2.8 GHz, 2.5 MB cache and four cores.
   a) Describe how the clock speed affects the performance of the computer. [2]
   b) Describe why having more cache memory will improve the performance of the computer. [2]
   c) State the purpose of the memory address register (MAR). [2]
   d) Explain how a multi-core CPU can improve the performance of the computer. [2]

2 a) State **one** item that might be held in the ROM in an embedded system inside a washing machine. [1]
   b) State **two** items of data that might be held in RAM in an embedded system inside a washing machine. [2]
   c) Describe **two** important features of an embedded system that make it appropriate for use in a car engine management system. [4]

3 a) Describe **three** types of operation carried out by the ALU. Give an example for each one. [6]
   b) Describe what happens at the fetch stage of the fetch–execute cycle. [3]

Answers on p. 103

1.2 Memory and storage

For a computer system to be useful, it needs storage for data and programs that:
+ are currently in use
+ can be accessed when required.

1.2.1 Primary storage (memory)

The need for primary storage   `REVISED` ◯

A computer system needs primary storage for any data that it needs to access quickly. This includes:
+ the start-up instructions
+ the operating system
+ programs that are running
+ any data associated with the operating system or programs.

Random access memory (RAM)   `REVISED` ◯

When the operating system or programs are loaded, they are copied from secondary storage, such as a hard disk drive (HDD), into RAM. Any data associated with these programs will also be stored in RAM so that the CPU can access both the data and the instructions.
+ Random access memory (RAM) is volatile, which means it needs power to maintain it. If the power is turned off the RAM loses its contents.
+ RAM holds the operating system and any applications and data currently in use by the computer.
+ The CPU can access RAM quickly – much faster than it can access secondary storage such as a hard disk drive.
+ The more RAM in a computer, the more programs and data it can run at the same time and the better the computer's performance.
+ RAM can be read from or written to.
+ RAM is also known as the main memory in the computer.

> Volatile means power is needed to maintain the contents; memory that does not require power to maintain the contents is called non-volatile.

Read-only memory (ROM)   `REVISED` ◯

+ Read-only memory (ROM) is non-volatile, which means it does not need power to maintain it. If the power is turned off ROM keeps its contents.
+ ROM provides storage for data and instructions needed to start up the computer (also known as the boot process).
+ ROM content is **read-only**, which means it cannot be overwritten.
+ The contents of ROM are written at manufacture or by a special process later on.

The difference between RAM and ROM   `REVISED` ◯

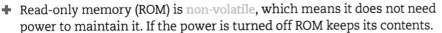

RAM	ROM
is volatile and needs power to maintain the content	is non-volatile and does not require power to maintain the content
is read and write – data can be read from and written to RAM by the computer	is read-only – the computer cannot overwrite its content
holds the operating system and any programs and data currently in use by the computer	holds the data and instructions required to start up (boot) the computer

Virtual memory

Running several programs at once, or running programs that use large amounts of data, can require more RAM than is available. However, the computer can assign a section of secondary storage to temporarily act like RAM. When RAM is fully utilised, data can be transferred between RAM and the hard disk drive. This section of secondary storage is called virtual memory.

> Virtual memory is a section of the hard drive that is used as if it were RAM to supplement the amount of main memory available to the computer.

✦ Any data from a running program that is not currently being used by the computer can be temporarily moved from RAM to virtual memory.

✦ When that data is required by the computer, it is moved back from virtual memory into RAM.

✦ Moving data between RAM and virtual memory is relatively slow – so using virtual memory slows down the performance of the computer.

✦ Adding more RAM reduces the need for virtual memory. If less data is held in virtual memory, then there are fewer slow data transfers between RAM and virtual memory.

✦ Therefore, adding more RAM improves the performance of the computer.

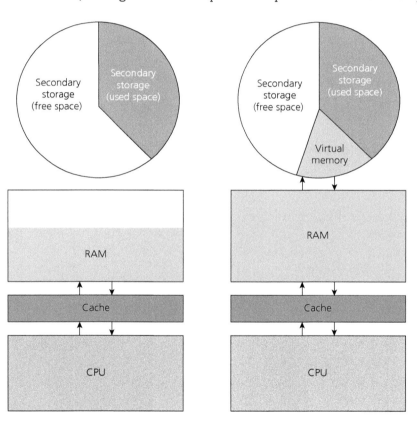

Figure 1.2.1 Virtual memory

Check your understanding

1 Why does a computer need both RAM and ROM?
2 Why is data transferred from secondary storage to RAM?
3 What is *virtual memory*?

Answers on p. 98

1.2.2 Secondary storage

The need for secondary storage

We need a way of saving our data and programs so that they are available the next time we switch on the computer. Secondary storage needs to be able to keep data safe and must be reliable and robust.

The choice of secondary storage depends on several factors.

Capacity	How much data does it need to hold?
Speed	How quickly can the data be accessed? Typically, access times to secondary storage are very slow compared to primary storage (main memory).
Portability	Does the data stored on the device need to be moved or transported? If so, the size, shape and weight of the medium is important.
Durability	How robust is the medium? Will it be damaged when moved around? Will it be used in a hostile environment subject to shocks or extreme conditions?
Reliability	Does it need to be used over and over again without failing?
Cost	What is the cost per GB of data stored? This is also an important factor where the media is being used to distribute data and will not be reused. CDs, for example, only cost pennies, but the cost per GB of storing data is higher than that for a magnetic hard disk drive.

Common types of storage

Magnetic storage

Magnetic storage mostly uses **hard disk drives (HDDs)**.
+ They are made of a stack of magnetic disks (or platters) that rotate.
+ A read/write head moves across the surface of the platters to read and write data.
+ Magnetic disks are reliable and cost-effective and provide high-capacity storage at low cost.

Solid-state storage

Solid-state storage uses a technology called flash memory. It is used in portable hand-held devices and increasingly in computers in the form of **solid-state drives (SSDs)**.

> **Flash memory** is a method of storing data using electronics.

SSDs have the following characteristics.
+ They use flash memory, so they have no moving parts; this means access to data is faster than for a magnetic hard disk drive, power requirements are low, and no noise or heat is generated.
+ They are robust, lightweight and compact, making them ideal for use in portable devices.
+ They have smaller capacity than magnetic hard disk drives and the cost per unit of storage is higher.
+ They are commonly used in tablet computers, mobile phones, cameras and general-purpose computers.
+ They have a limited number of write cycles; once that limit is reached, the drive will not allow any more writes and will become read-only.

Optical storage

+ **Optical storage** devices use the properties of light to store data.
+ The most common optical storage media are optical disks – CDs, DVDs and Blu-Ray disks.
+ They work by reflecting laser light onto the surface of the rotating disk and reading the reflections as 1s or 0s.
+ CD-ROMs and DVD-ROMs are read-only media.
+ CD-R and DVD-R are write-once/read many times media.

+ CD-RW and DVD-RW are rewriteable media.
+ Blu-Ray disks use a blue laser light that can detect data stored at a higher density than CDs and DVDs.
+ Blu-Ray disks have a much higher capacity than CDs and DVDs, making them ideal for storing and distributing high-definition video films or large amounts of data.
+ Blu-Ray disks can be formatted with up to four layers for very high capacity.
+ Optical media are low cost and robust, making them an ideal way to distribute data.

The advantages and disadvantages of different storage devices

REVISED ⬤

Capacity and cost of storage media

Media	Capacity	Cost per GB
magnetic hard disk	up to 15TB	3p
SSD	250MB up to 2TB	15p
DVD	8.5GB	9p
Blu-Ray	50GB	6p
CD	700MB	23p

CDs are very cheap to buy and can store small files for a low overall cost but are the most expensive per gigabyte.

For larger files, higher capacity media are required and larger storage requirements can be met more cost-effectively by a magnetic hard disk drive.

Speed

Storage type	Data transfer rates
SSD	Fastest
magnetic hard disk	↓
Blu-Ray disk	
DVD	
CD	Slowest

Portability, durability and reliability

Media	Portability	Durability	Reliability
SSD	small, with low power requirements very portable	no moving parts, so are not subject to damage from sudden shocks	medium is reliable and will hold data safely for a long time before failure
magnetic hard disk	moving parts, so higher power requirements than SSD available as external drives powered from a USB	subject to damage from being dropped or from exposure to magnetic fields	ideal for medium term storage with a reliable life of 5–7 years motors and heads are subject to failure over time or from excessive use or mishandling
CD; DVD; Blu-Ray	light and small very portable – can even be sent through the post	reasonably robust and resistant to shocks easily damaged by mishandling and scratches	CDs and DVDs will start to fail after 10 years, while Blu-Ray will fail after 20 years

Fragmentation

During use, files can be stored in several locations scattered over the surface of a drive. Since magnetic hard disks have to move heads and rotate the platters to read these files, the time taken to access a file is increased dramatically if the data is fragmented. Defragmenting the HDD reorganises the data so that it can be accessed much more quickly.

SSDs do not have any moving parts so, while they do become fragmented, there is no need to defragment them since access times are not affected by fragmentation. In fact, because SSDs have limited read/write cycles, defragmenting would shorten the life time of the drive.

> **Exam tip**
>
> Be careful when answering questions about the choice or suitability of storage media – answers such as 'faster', 'cheaper' or 'more reliable' are not enough without further explanation.

> **Check your understanding**
>
> 4 What is stored on the hard disk in a computer?
> 5 Identify **three** factors to consider when choosing a secondary storage device.
>
> **Answers on p. 98**

1.2.3 Units

Why data needs to be converted to binary to be stored

Computers use switches to store data and these switches can be in one of two states: ON or OFF. These switches are called transistors.

We use these two states to represent 1 and 0.

Because of this, we convert all data and instructions into **binary**, which uses the two digits 1 and 0.

The units of data storage

+ Each stored binary digit is called a bit (binary digit).
+ A group of 8 bits is called a **byte**.
+ Half a byte, 4 bits, is called a **nibble**.

The symbol for bit is **b** and for bytes is **B**; make sure that you use the correct symbol.

> **Exam tip**
>
> In some sources you might see these units in multiples of 1024 but you should use 1000 in the examination. If you do use 1024 you will not be penalised.

4 b (bits)	1 nibble
8 b (bits)	1 B (byte)
1000 B	1 KB (kilobyte)
1000 KB	1 MB (megabyte)
1000 MB	1 GB (gigabyte)
1000 GB	1 TB (terabyte)
1000 TB	1 PB (petabyte)

> **Worked example**
>
> A file is 3.6 MB. What is its size in bytes?
>
> $3.6 \times 1000 \times 1000 = 3\,600\,000$ bytes.

Data capacity and calculation of data capacity requirements

It is important to be able to calculate the required data capacity when choosing storage media.

To do this, we add up the estimated file size for each of the files we need to store.

> **Exam tip**
>
> You do not need to remember any typical file sizes; this information will be supplied as part of the question.

Worked example

Some typical file sizes are shown in this table.

File type	Approximate size
one-page word-processed document with no images	100 KB
postcard-sized photograph	6 MB
three-minute MP3 music track	6 MB
one-minute MPEG video	50 MB

Calculating the storage space required for …

20 pages of word-processed text	20 × 100 KB = 2000 KB	2 MB
five postcard-sized images	5 × 6 MB = 30 MB	30 MB
30 minutes of MP3 music	30 mins ÷ 3 mins = 10 tracks; 10 × 6 MB = 60 MB	60 MB
10 minute MPEG video	10 × 50 MB	500 MB
	Total storage space required	**592 MB**

> **Exam tip**
>
> When calculating the size of a file, there will be some metadata that describes the data and how it can be used to create the original object, image, sound or text. In most cases this is quite small compared to the original file and can be ignored. Rounding up a calculation may be sufficient to account for the metadata in most cases.

Check your understanding

6 How many megabytes is 2.1 GB?

7 Calculate how much storage space we would require for 15 postcard-sized images and 60 minutes of MP3 music using the typical file size data in the worked example above.

Answers on p. 98

1.2.4 Data storage

All data (including numbers, characters, images and sound) are represented in binary on a computer.

In binary, we have just two symbols, 0 and 1.

In binary, the column values are twice as big as the previous one as we go from right to left:

128	64	32	16	8	4	2	1

The leftmost digit in binary is called the **most significant bit (MSB)** and the rightmost digit the **least significant bit (LSB)**. In an 8-bit number this means the MSB has a denary (decimal) value of 128 and the LSB a denary value of 1.

Converting between denary and binary

Binary to denary

To convert a **binary number into denary**:

✚ use the table and write the binary number into the columns making sure the LSB is in the rightmost column (value 1)

✚ add together the column values for every column with a 1 in the binary number.

Worked example

To convert 1011001 from binary to denary:

128	64	32	16	8	4	2	1
	1	0	1	1	0	0	1

We have:

64 + 16 + 8 + 1 = 89

Denary to binary

To convert a **denary number to binary**:

✚ decide if each column value, starting with the MSB, is smaller than or equal to the decimal number
  ✚ if it is smaller than or equal to, we record 1 in the table, and subtract that column value from the new decimal number; we then check if that new number is smaller than the next column value
  ✚ if it is not smaller, we check the original decimal number against the next column, and so on
✚ we continue this process until we are left with the 1s column.

Worked example

To convert 97 into binary:

Is 128 smaller than 97? No, so we record 0 in the 128 column.

128	64	32	16	8	4	2	1
0							

Is 64 smaller than 97? Yes, so we record 1 in the 64 column and subtract 64 from 97.

The new number is 97 − 64 = 33

128	64	32	16	8	4	2	1
0	1						

Is 32 smaller than 33? Yes, so we record 1 in the 32 column and subtract 32 from 33.

The new number is 33 − 32 = 1

128	64	32	16	8	4	2	1
0	1	1					

We now check against 16, 8, 4, 2 and record 0 in each of those columns.

128	64	32	16	8	4	2	1
0	1	1	0	0	0	0	

We are left with 1, so we record 1 in the 1 column.

128	64	32	16	8	4	2	1
0	1	1	0	0	0	0	1

We do not need to write down the leading 0s, so 97 in denary is 1100001 in binary.

Exam tip

Check your answer by converting the binary back to denary; in this case, 64 + 32 + 1 = 97.

Exam tip

In the exam, you are expected to deal with binary numbers with up to eight digits. But you can expect to see binary digits with fewer than eight digits. In the computer, the leading 0s are recorded but, when written down, they do not need to be.

Exam tip

In the exam, show your working by using the table and showing the key subtractions.

8 Convert the following binary numbers to denary.
   a) 1011
   b) 110011
   c) 1001100
9 Convert the following denary numbers to binary.
   a) 74
   b) 144
   c) 85

Answers on p. 98

Adding two 8-bit binary integers

REVISED

Adding binary numbers is similar to adding in denary. When we add 1s together and get 2 or more we generate a carry to the next column.

There are four possibilities.

Sum	Write down	Carry to the next column
0 + 0	0	none
1 + 0	1	none
1 + 1	0	1
1 + 1 + 1	1	1

Worked example

1011 + 1111

```
      1   0   1   1
+     1   1   1   1
   ─────────────────
   1  1   0   1   0
   ─────────────────
      1   1   1   1
```

So, 1011 + 1111 = 11010

Check by converting to denary:

11 + 15 = 26 ✓

Exam tip

It is always worth taking a few moments to check the binary addition by converting it to denary.

Worked example

11000101 + 11100011

```
    1   1   0   0   0   1   0   1
+   1   1   1   0   0   0   1   1
 ───────────────────────────────
 1  0   1   0   1   0   0   0
 ───────────────────────────────
    1               1   1   1
```

We have a carry into the ninth column, but we can only represent 8 bits, so it is lost.
 ✦ The result will not fit into 8 bits.
 ✦ This is called overflow and means the result will be incorrect.

Converting to denary, using the 8 bits available, we get 197 + 227 = 168, which is clearly incorrect.
 ✦ Overflow errors can generate further logical errors in a program because the result is not as expected.
 ✦ This may lead to incorrect results from the program.
 ✦ The program may crash if it cannot deal with the overflow digit.

Check your understanding

10 Complete the following binary additions.

    a) 110011 + 11101

    b) 100010 + 100111

    c) 111000 + 11110

Answers on p. 98

Converting between denary and hexadecimal

REVISED ●

Computer scientists use another number system based on 16: **hexadecimal** (hex for short).

We already have symbols for 10 digits in the denary system, 0–9.

We need another six symbols to represent the denary values 10–15.

We use the letters A–F for this.

Denary value	10	11	12	13	14	15
Hex symbol	A	B	C	D	E	F

The hex system is based on 16, so the column values are:

16	1

> **Exam tip**
>
> You are only required to work with two digit hexadecimal numbers for the exam.

Denary to hexadecimal

To convert **denary numbers to hexadecimal** we:

+ check if 16 will divide into the number
+ if it does, we write down how many times using the correct hexadecimal symbol in the 16s column
+ we then convert the remainder into its hexadecimal symbol and write it in the 1s column.

> **Worked example**
>
> Convert 185 into hexadecimal.
>
> 185 divided by 16 is 11 remainder 9 ◄—— You can check this: $11 \times 16 = 176$ and $185 - 176 = 9$
>
> The hex symbol for 11 is B.
>
> The hex symbol for 9 is the same, 9.
>
> 185 in hexadecimal is B9.

Hexadecimal to denary

To convert **hexadecimal numbers to denary** we:

+ convert the individual symbols to their denary equivalent
+ multiply the denary values by the column values – either 16 or 1
+ add the results.

> **Worked example**
>
> Convert CE from hexadecimal to denary.
>
> | 16 | 1 |
> |---|---|
> | C | E |
>
> C is equivalent to denary 12.
>
> E is equivalent to denary 14.
>
> $(12 \times 16) + (14 \times 1) = 192 + 14 = 206$.

23

11 Convert the following denary numbers to hexadecimal.

   a) 91   **b)** 173   **c)** 247

12 Convert the following hexadecimal numbers to denary.

   a) 5A   **b)** AB   **c)** B7

Answers on p. 98

Converting between binary and hexadecimal

REVISED

Computer scientists use hexadecimal because binary numbers are more difficult to work with and remember. For example, 11011011 in hexadecimal is DB. This is far easier to remember and communicate without introducing errors.

Hexadecimal to binary

To convert from **hexadecimal to binary**:

+ convert each hex symbol to the equivalent binary
+ combine both 4-bit binary numbers (nibbles) into an 8-bit binary number.

Worked example

Convert CF in hexadecimal to binary.

Hex	C	F
Denary	12	15
Binary	1100	1111

CF in hexadecimal is 1100111 in binary.

Binary to hexadecimal

To convert from **binary to hexadecimal**:

+ if the binary number has fewer than 8 bits, add leading 0s to make it 8 bits
+ split into two nibbles
+ convert each nibble to the hex equivalent.

Worked example

1011101

Add leading 0s to make it 8 bits and divide into two nibbles.

0101 1101

Binary	0101	1101
Denary	5	13
Hex	5	D

1011101 in binary is 5D in hexadecimal.

Exam tip

This may be easier by converting to denary before converting to hex.

13 Convert the following hexadecimal numbers to binary.

   a) 8C   **b)** 5B   **c)** FE

14 Convert the following binary numbers to hexadecimal.

   a) 10100011   **b)** 11001010   **c)** 1001110

Answers on p. 98

Binary shifts

Moving the binary digits to the left or right is called a **binary shift**.

Moving to the left multiplies the value by 2 for each place the value is shifted.

Moving to the right divides the number by 2 for each place the value is shifted.

Worked examples

Starting with the binary number 10110, which has the denary value 22.

128	64	32	16	8	4	2	1
			1	0	1	1	0

If we shift the number one place to the left we get:

128	64	32	16	8	4	2	1
		1	0	1	1	0	0

The equivalent denary value is now 44; that is, multiplied by 2.

If we shift two places to the left we get:

128	64	32	16	8	4	2	1
	1	0	1	1	0	0	0

which has the denary value 88; that is, the original number, 22, multiplied by 4.

+ Shifting left n places multiplies the number by 2^n.
+ If we shift too far to the left, we eventually need a ninth bit to store the 1 in the MSB.
+ The number cannot be stored in the available bits, creating an **overflow error**.

Starting with our original number:

128	64	32	16	8	4	2	1
			1	0	1	1	0

Shifting one place to the right we get:

128	64	32	16	8	4	2	1
				1	0	1	1

The denary value is now 11; that is, 22 divided by 2.

If we shift the number two places to the right, however, we have a problem; we lose a 1:

128	64	32	16	8	4	2	1
					1	0	1

The new value is 5, but 11 ÷ 2 = 5.5

We have lost some information, which has led to a **lack of precision**.

Shifting the number so that we lose a 1 causes an error.
+ Shifting too far to the left when the MSB is a 1 means that we lose that 1 and we have an overflow error.
+ Shifting too far to the right when the LSB is a 1 means that we lose that 1 and we have a lack of precision.

Check your understanding

15 Apply the shifts described using 8 bits. State the denary value before and after the shift and the effect of the shift.
   a) 1001 shift two places to the left.
   b) 1100 shift one place to the right.
   c) 11100 shift three places to the left.
   d) 1101 shift one place to the right.

Answers on p. 98

The use of binary codes to represent characters

When you press the keys on a keyboard, the computer registers this as a **binary code**.

This code can then be used to identify and display a character on screen or for printing.

Character sets

+ The **character set** of a computer is a list of all the characters available to the computer.
+ It is important that computer systems all agree on these codes and there are some agreed standards.

ASCII

The ASCII system was designed to provide codes for:

+ all the main English alphabet characters, both upper and lower case
+ all the numeric symbols 0–9
+ the main punctuations symbols and space
+ some non-printable control codes.

In all, 128 codes are required using 7 bits.

Some ASCII codes are:

Binary	Denary	Character
0100000	32	'space'
1000001	65	A
1000010	66	B
1000011	67	C
1100001	97	a
1111010	122	z
0110000	48	0
0110001	49	1

The ASCII codes for the main alphabetic characters are allocated to the uppercase characters in sequence, starting with 'A' as 65 and 'B' as one more at 66, and so on. The lowercase characters start with 'a' as 97, 'b' as 98, and so on. This means that when we sort text, 'Z' comes before 'a'.

For example, if the following animals written as Goat, Bear, ape, Zebra, deer are sorted using ASCII values, they will be in the order:

Bear, Goat, Zebra, ape, deer

Extended ASCII

The original ASCII codes used an eighth bit for error checking.

As the need for more characters became necessary this error checking bit was used to extend the character set making 256 characters available.

Unicode

Unicode was developed to use 16 bits initially, extending the number of characters to 2^{16} or 65 536.

In order to represent a wider range of language symbols, graphical symbols and emoji, this has been extended to 32 bits, making billions of characters available.

The original ASCII codes have been retained in Unicode, making ASCII effectively a subset of Unicode.

Character set	Number of bits	Number of characters	Examples
ASCII	7	128	upper and lowercase, numbers, punctuation, some control characters
extended ASCII	8	256	as above, plus non-English characters and mathematical symbols
unicode	16/32 bits	65000/2 billion +	as above, plus all known language characters and different characters including wingdings and emoji

The size of a text file can be calculated using:

number of characters × number of bits per character

> **Worked example**
>
> A text file with 200 characters using 32-bit Unicode.
>
> 200 × 32 = 6400 bits.
>
> Dividing by 8 to get this in bytes we get 800 bytes.

How an image is represented as pixels and in binary

Images are represented on screen as a series of **pixels**.
+ A pixel is the smallest element of an image – these are the dots that make up the image on screen or in a printout.
+ Pixels are stored in a computer as binary codes.

A simple image can be made up of black and white blocks.

Using 1 to for black and 0 for white, we can represent this image using just 8 bytes.

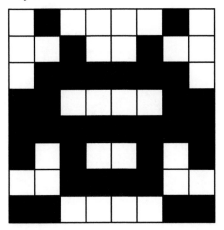

0	1	0	0	0	0	1	0
0	0	1	0	0	1	0	0
0	1	1	1	1	1	1	0
1	1	0	0	0	0	1	1
1	1	1	1	1	1	1	1
1	0	1	0	0	1	0	1
0	0	1	1	1	1	0	0
1	1	0	0	0	0	1	1

Figure 1.2.2 A simple black and white image (left) with binary codes (right)

If we use four colours we need binary codes for four colours.

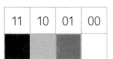

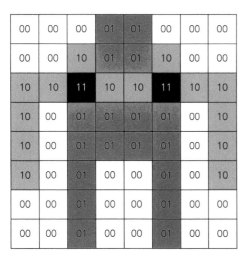

Figure 1.2.3 Image of four-colour space invader with binary codes

In this case we need two bytes to represent each row, a total of 16 bytes for the image.

The number of bits used for each pixel determines how many colours each pixel can represent.

With 1 bit for each pixel we have just two possibilities: 0 or 1. This means a pixel can only be one of two colours.

With 2 bits for each pixel we have four possibilities, 00, 01, 10, 11. This means we can use four colours.

To store more colours we need more bits per pixel.
+ 3 bits to store 8 (2^3) colours per pixel.
+ 8 bits to store 256 (2^8) colours per pixel.

Image metadata

The data for the image is stored as a series of binary numbers.

To make sense of this and reproduce the original image the computer needs to know how to interpret the binary data.

This information about the image is called **metadata** and is stored as part of the file along with the data for the image.

Metadata includes information such as:
+ the number of bits per pixel (the colour depth)
+ the size of the image in bits
+ the resolution of the image in dots per inch (DPI).

The effect of colour depth and resolution on image quality and size

Colour depth is the number of bits used per pixel.
+ The more bits per pixel, the larger the range of colours we can have in the image.
+ The more colours available, the better the representation of the image.
+ The more colours, the more bits per pixel needed, and the more data to store.
+ The higher the colour depth, the larger the file needed to store the image.

The **resolution** of an image is the number of pixels per unit of distance – dots per inch (DPI).

✚ The more pixels per inch, the greater the detail stored.
✚ This enables us to enlarge the image more without it becoming pixelated.
✚ The more dots or pixels per inch, the more data to store, meaning the image file is larger.

Pixelated means the image becomes blocky when enlarged.

To calculate the size of an image file, we need to know the colour depth and the width and height of the image in pixels:

file size = colour depth × image height (pixel) × image width (pixel)

Worked example

Calculate the file size for a 16-bit image that is 1500 pixels high and 1200 pixels wide.

File size = 16 × 1500 × 1200
       = 28 800 000 bits

In bytes this is:

28 800 000 ÷ 8 = 3 600 000 B
          = 3.6 MB

There would also be some metadata to enable the computer to reproduce the image, which would add a small amount to the file size. However, 3.6 MB represents a reasonable estimate of the file size.

Check your understanding

16 How many colours can be represented using 6 bits?
17 Calculate the file size for a 32-bit image that is 2000 pixels high and 3000 pixels wide.

Answers on p. 98

How sound can be sampled and stored in digital form

Sounds are a series of vibrations that continuously vary and can take any value – this means they are **analogue**.

In order to store this on a computer, sound is sampled at regular intervals by a device that converts analogue to digital signals and the digital values are stored as binary.

The effect of sample rate, duration and bit depth on sound quality and file size

The **sample rate** is the number of samples taken per second measured in hertz (Hz). One sample per second = 1 Hz.

✚ If we sample more frequently, we will get a better approximation of the original sound.
✚ Each sample requires a certain amount of data, so more samples means a larger file to store the data.

The **bit depth** is the number of bits used to store each sampled value.

✚ The more bits we use, the more accurately we can represent the data for that sample point, providing a better representation of the original sound.
✚ The more bits we use to store each data point, the larger the file needed to store the data.

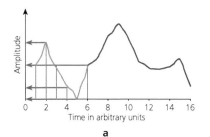 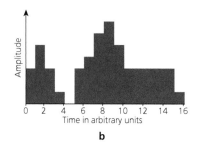 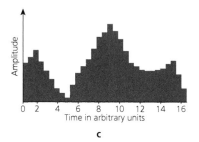

a   b   c

Figure 1.2.4 Sound is sampled at set time intervals **(a)**; this creates a digital sound that can be replayed by the computer **(b)**; higher sample rates and bit depths produce a better approximation of the original sound **(c)**

Exam tip

Do not confuse sample rate and bit depth. The bit depth is how much data is stored for each sample point. Sample rate is how frequently the sample is taken.

The size of the file needed to store sound data depends on the:
+ sample rate
+ duration
+ bit depth
+ number of channels (for example, stereo sound uses two channels).

size of file = sample rate × duration × bit depth × number of channels

---

Worked example

A stereo sound is sampled using two channels at 48 KHz for 2 minutes at a depth of 32 bits. Calculate the file size.

48 000 × 32 = 1 536 000 bits per second.

The sample lasts 120 seconds.

1 536 000 × 120 = 184 320 000 bits.

Divide by 8 to get the number of bytes.

184 320 000 ÷ 8 = 23 040 000 bytes.

Divide by 1 000 000 for megabytes.

23 040 000 ÷ 1 000 000 = 23.04 MB.

There are two channels.

23.04 × 2 = **46.08 MB**

Check your understanding

18 How do bit depth and sample rate affect the size of the file used to store a digital sound?

19 Calculate the file size for a sound sampled on one channel at 22 KHz for 20 seconds at a depth of 8 bits.

Answers on p. 98

1.2.5 Compression

When transmitting files, storing very large files or storing a large number of files, we often need to compress the data to make it smaller.

Lossy compression

REVISED ○

Lossy compression is where some data is permanently removed to make the file smaller.
+ With sound there are frequencies that are inaudible to humans and we will not miss these.
+ In images there are frequently large blocks of very similar colours that can be combined without significantly affecting the quality of the image.

In these cases we can safely remove some data.

Once this data is removed it cannot be replaced. A file compressed using lossy compression cannot be restored to its original quality.

Lossless compression

REVISED ○

Lossless compression uses techniques to compress files without losing any of the original data.
+ In documents, we cannot afford to lose words or characters without altering the original document.
+ Computer programs will only work if all the code is there.

Algorithms look for patterns in the data so that repeated data items only need to be stored once, together with information about how to restore them.
+ None of the data is removed.
+ The original file can be restored.

Check your understanding

20 Describe what is meant by:
   a) lossy compression
   b) lossless compression.
21 Describe when you would use lossless compression.

Answers on p. 98

Exam checklist

In this chapter you learned about:

Primary storage (memory)
+ The need for primary storage
+ The purpose of RAM in a computer system
+ The purpose of ROM in a computer system
+ The difference between RAM and ROM
+ Virtual memory

Secondary storage
+ The need for secondary storage
+ Common types of storage
+ The advantages and disadvantages of different storage devices

Units
+ The units of data storage
+ How data needs to be converted into a binary format to be processed by a computer
+ Data capacity and calculation of data capacity requirements

Data storage
+ Converting between denary, binary and hexadecimal
+ How to add two 8-bit binary integers together and explain how overflow errors occur
+ Binary shifts
+ The use of binary codes to represent characters
+ Character sets, the relationship between the number of bits per character and the number of characters in a character set
+ How an image is represented as pixels and in binary
+ Image metadata
+ The effect of colour depth and resolution on image quality and size
+ How sound can be sampled and stored in digital form
+ The effect of sample rate, duration and bit depth on sound quality and file size

Compression
+ The need for compression
+ Types of compression (lossy and lossless)

1 Write definitions of ROM and RAM and what data they hold.
2 Write a description of virtual memory and how its use affects the speed of the computer.
3 List the factors that affect the quality of an image file and how that affects the size of the file used to store it.
4 List the factors that affect the quality of a sampled sound file and how that affects the size of the file used to store it.

Exam-style questions

1 a) Convert the denary value 69 to binary held in a single byte. [1]
  b) Convert the denary value 108 to a hexadecimal value. [1]
  c) Add together the following two binary numbers. [3]

$$
\begin{array}{ccccccc}
 & 1 & 1 & 0 & 1 & 0 & 1 \\
+ & 1 & 0 & 0 & 1 & 1 & 1 \\
\hline
\end{array}
$$

  d) For the binary number 100111:
    i) convert to denary [1]
    ii) show the result of applying a shift of one place to the left [1]
    iii) explain what would happen if we applied a shift of one place to the right. [2]

2 a) State what is meant by *bit depth* for a digital sound sample. [1]
  b) Explain how the bit depth affects the quality of the sampled sound. [2]
  c) A sound is sampled at a rate of 41 KHz for 15 seconds at a bit depth 16 on one channel. Calculate the size of the file required to store the sample. [4]

3 a) State what is meant by *colour depth*. [1]
  b) State what is meant by *image resolution*. [1]
  c) Explain how colour depth and image resolution affect the quality of the stored image. [4]
  d) Explain why lossy compression is suitable for image files. [2]

4 Explain what is meant by the *character set* of a computer. [2]

Answers on p. 103

A computer network is two or more computer devices linked together to communicate and to share resources and data.

A range of devices may be connected to a network including:
+ smartphones
+ smart televisions
+ gaming consoles
+ printers
+ security cameras
+ smart speakers
+ home appliances and control systems.

Advantages of computer networks include:
⊕ ability to share resources and devices
⊕ ease of exchanging data
⊕ communication between users
⊕ centralised management in larger networks, for example to update software and control access.

Disadvantages of computer networks include:
⊖ additional cost of necessary hardware
⊖ malware can spread throughout the network from one infection
⊖ larger systems require staff to manage the system.

1.3.1 Networks and topologies

Types of network

Local area network (LAN)	Wide area network (WAN)
covers a small geographical area	covers a large geographical area, often worldwide locations
the computers and devices are usually located on a single site, such as a home, an office, a school	the computers and devices are distributed around several locations often quite distant from each other, for example by a multinational business or a national government
the hardware is usually owned and maintained by the person or organisation that uses it	the connections are often leased from a telecommunications company, for example cable, satellite, telephone links

A WAN is often a group of LANs connected together by a telecommunication service.

> **Exam tip**
>
> You might see questions asking what type of network is appropriate or suitable for a given situation. You should justify your choice by matching the features of these networks to the situation.

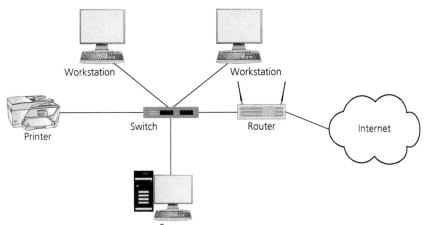

Figure 1.3.1 Basic LAN network

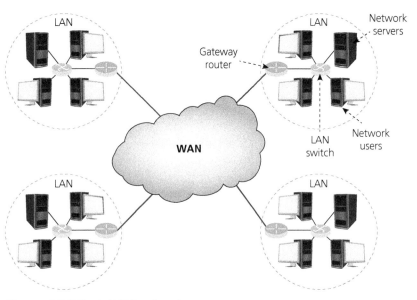

Figure 1.3.2 Basic WAN network

Factors that affect the performance of networks

REVISED ●

Bandwidth

Bandwidth is the amount of data that can be transmitted in a given time. It is usually measured in megabits per second (Mbps).

The higher the bandwidth the more data that can be transmitted per second.

The bandwidth depends on the equipment and transmission media (cables) used on the network.

> **Exam tip**
>
> The choice of transmission media is determined by the situation. Fibre may have the largest bandwidth, but it is also the most expensive and most difficult to install.

Number of users

The bandwidth is shared between users.
+ The more users there are, the greater the chance of congestion, and data will be queued before transmission.
+ Activities such as streaming video use a lot of bandwidth, leaving less bandwidth for other users.

Transmission media

Data is transmitted on a network using cables or wirelessly.

The bandwidth for these media differs significantly.

Media	Bandwidth
Wi-Fi	up to 300 Mbps
copper Ethernet cable	100 Mbps up to 1 Gbps
fibre-optic cable	up to 1 Tbps

Error rates

When there is a lot of data on a network, data packets can collide causing a transmission error.

If other sources, such as nearby radio signals, interfere with the network they can cause a transmission error.

If transmission errors occur, the data has to be re-sent increasing network traffic.

The error rate is the number of errors that occur within a given period of time.

> **Check your understanding**
>
> 1 Describe the characteristics of a WAN.
> 2 Describe **two** disadvantages of a network.
> 3 Describe **two** factors that affect the bandwidth available to an individual network user.
>
> **Answers on p. 99**

Client–server and peer-to-peer networks

REVISED ⬤

There are two main ways of organising a computer network: client–server and peer-to-peer.

Client–server networks

There are two types of computer on a client–server network.

Clients are the computers providing access for the network users. They:
+ request services and resources such as software and files from a server
+ do not normally store any data.

Servers are the computers providing services for the network. They:
+ are high-end computers offering high performance but at high cost
+ often provide specialised services for the network including:
    + **file servers** to store users' documents and files; this means that they can be accessed from any computer on the network
    + **authentication servers** to check whether a username and password match those stored in a database, and then control the resources that a user can access
    + **application servers** to run programs across the network
    + **web servers** to store and share web pages
    + **print servers** to manage printing across the network
    + **mail servers** to store and handle email.

Client–server is the most common network organisation and is used in various organisations with large numbers of computers where users need access to the same range of software or files.

Advantages of client–server networks include:
⊕ managed centrally
⊕ files accessed from any client
⊕ central backup
⊕ software and security is managed by network managers
⊕ client activity can be monitored
⊕ access levels can be set so that users only have access to files they should have
⊕ security and passwords are managed centrally.

Disadvantages of client–server networks include:
- ⊖ if a server fails, then none of the users have access to the service it provided, such as files and software
- ⊖ server hardware can be very expensive
- ⊖ the whole network can be subject to an attack or malware infection via the server.

Peer-to-peer networks

In peer-to-peer networks:
- ✦ the computers all have equal status
- ✦ all computers are connected directly or indirectly to each other
- ✦ files and folders can be accessed by other peers on the network.

This is the model for small organisations or home networks.
Typical uses include:
- ✦ wireless printing from connected devices, such as laptop, tablet, phone
- ✦ file sharing from device to device
- ✦ audio streaming to connected speakers
- ✦ sharing internet connections.

Advantages of peer-to-peer networks include:
- ⊕ easy to set up, such as home Wi-Fi
- ⊕ no need for expensive hardware such as a high-end server
- ⊕ if one device fails it does not affect the other devices.

Disadvantages of peer-to-peer networks include:
- ⊖ no central management or support – software and security updates have to be carried out on each device
- ⊖ no centralised backup
- ⊖ duplicate copies of files on the peer devices – including out-of-date versions of documents
- ⊖ peers may go offline while being accessed – they may lose connection or simply be turned off.

Check your understanding

4 Describe the differences between the clients on a peer-to-peer network and on a client – server network.

5 Describe **two** disadvantages of a client–server network.

6 Explain why a peer-to-peer system is suitable for a home network.

Answers on p. 99

Hardware needed to connect computers into a LAN

REVISED ○

Network interface controller (NIC)

A network interface controller is required to connect a device to a network. It receives data from and sends data to a network.
- ✦ The NIC is often integrated into the motherboard of a computer device.
- ✦ It formats the data ready to be sent on to a network using the appropriate protocols.
- ✦ The most common types of NIC are an Ethernet port to connect to a wired network and a radio transmitter to connect to a wireless network.
- ✦ Every NIC has a **Media Access Control (MAC) address**, a unique identifier added at the manufacturing stage. The MAC address is used when transmitting data around a network.

Transmission media

Copper Ethernet cable	Fibre-optic cable	Radio waves
copper cable made up of eight wires twisted together in pairs to reduce interference from other signals	made of thin glass strands (fibres) that transmit data as light pulses do not suffer from interference	use of radio waves is controlled by governments; the frequencies used are 2.4 GHz and 5 GHz Bluetooth uses ultra-high frequency radio waves subject to interference from physical objects and other sources of electromagnetic radiation
bandwidth of between 100 Mbps and 1 Gbps	bandwidth of up to 100 Tbps	bandwidth of up to 300 Mbps
can work over distances of up to 100 m	can work over distances of 100 kilometres or more	Wi-Fi suitable for distances of up to 100 m outside with no interference, or 50 m inside Bluetooth suitable for very short distances
most PCs have built in Ethernet ports	do not break easily often used to connect WANs over large distances or provide internet services to communities used in connections that cross oceans to connect different continents	used to connect devices that are relatively close to each other most devices have built in wireless connectivity (no additional wiring required)

Wireless access point (WAP)

WAP is a piece of hardware that connects to the network allowing Wi-Fi devices to connect.
+ WAPs broadcast a name (**Service Set Identifier, SSID**) so that devices can connect to it.
+ The wireless data it receives is then sent on to the main network.
+ Usually connected to the network via a switch using an Ethernet cable but may be also connect via another WAP.

Switches

A network switch is hardware that connects multiple devices together to form a wired network.

A switch stores the MAC address of every connected device in order to be able to direct data it receives to the correct node.

> A **node** is any device connected to the network.
>
> **Packets** are small chunks of data that are sent separately, and then reassembled by the destination device.

Routers

A router is hardware that connects networks together, for example to connect a LAN to the internet.
+ Uses the destination IP address to send data to the correct location.
+ If the destination is not on the local network the data is passed to the connected network.
+ Routers collect data about all the available routes to transmit data then select the most appropriate route for each packet of data.

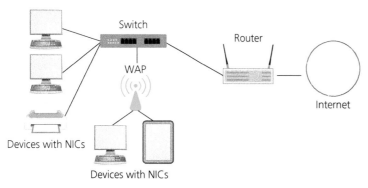

Figure **1.3.3** Basic network diagram

Check your understanding

7 Describe **two** advantages of fibre-optic cable over Ethernet cable to supply internet services to customers in a small town.

8 Explain how a switch identifies a client in order to send it data.

9 Explain what an SSID is.

Answers on p. 99

The internet as a worldwide collection of computer networks

REVISED

The internet is a worldwide collection of computers linked together as a WAN.

+ The set of rules to make sure these computers all work together is called the **Internet Protocol (IP)**.
+ The IP address is used to send data from one device to another. Every computer on the internet has a unique IP address.

Websites have IP addresses, such as 212.58.244.26, but since this is hard to remember we use a **Uniform Resource Locator (URL)**, such as www.hoddereducation.co.uk, to identify websites.

+ The URL includes a **domain name**, such as hoddereducation.co.uk in the example above.

Domain Name Server (DNS)

The **Domain Name Server**, or domain name system, keeps a record of the IP addresses of the servers that host the websites.

+ When a user requests a URL the DNS looks for a matching IP address.
+ If it does not have an address it asks another DNS.
+ This process continues until the IP is found or an error message is returned if the URL is unknown.

Hosting

An **internet host** is a company that stores files and makes them available to devices over the internet.

All websites are hosted on a web server that responds to HTTP and HTTPS requests by returning web pages.

Anyone can set up a web server, but usually they will use a web hosting company.

A web hosting company will charge a fee for the service and will often include domain name registration on the DNS, regular backups and service guarantees.

The cloud

The cloud is a term that refers to the storage of files and provision of software via the internet.

The cloud is a network of servers storing data and running applications in data centres around the world.

Advantages of cloud computing include:
⊕ files and applications can be accessed from anywhere providing there is an internet connection
⊕ applications are always up to date
⊕ updates are provided by the cloud providers so there is no need to update individual computers
⊕ storage is flexible and can be upgraded for a price
⊕ backup and security is carried out by the cloud service provider
⊕ data can be shared with others anywhere in the world.

Disadvantages of cloud computing include:
⊖ an internet connection is required
⊖ users have no control over security
⊖ it is unclear who actually owns the stored data
⊖ prices and terms of service can be changed with little or no notice.

Star and mesh network topologies

 REVISED

The way in which devices are organised on a network is called its topology.

Star network

The most common network layout is where each device is connected to a central point, a switch.
✚ Found in large organisations such as businesses and schools.
✚ Typical of a home network where all the devices connect to a central router with a wireless access point.

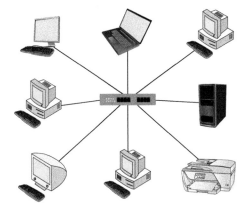

Figure 1.3.4 Star network topology

Advantages of a star network include:
⊕ robust and reliable since every device has its own connection to the central node
⊕ minimises traffic since data is only directed to the intended node
⊕ robust because the failure of one connection does not affect the others.

Disadvantages of a star network include:
⊖ wired star networks require a lot of cabling, which can be intrusive and expensive
⊖ if the central switch fails, the whole network fails.

> **Exam tip**
>
> The diagram for a star network looks very much like the diagram for a client–server network. The term 'star' refers to the way the devices are physically connected, while client–server refers to how they communicate. Try not to confuse the two.

Mesh network

In a mesh network, all the devices are connected directly or indirectly to each other. There is no central switch. Computers store their own data and also pass on data from other devices.

In a full mesh network, every device is connected directly to every other device. In a partial mesh network, direct connections only exist between some of the devices, although all devices are able to communicate with one another indirectly.

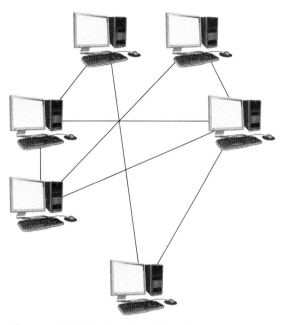

Figure 1.3.5 Mesh network topology

Advantages of mesh networks include:
⊕ very robust with no single point of failure, so used when reliable communication is essential such as in military or emergency service applications
⊕ in the event of a failure of a communication route, other routes are available
⊕ multiple communication routes mean that data can be transmitted simultaneously, allowing high volumes of traffic
⊕ wireless mesh networks are relatively cheap and simple to set up and to extend the range of the network.

Disadvantages of mesh networks include:
⊖ wired full mesh networks require vast numbers of connections and are very expensive and impractical
⊖ the complexity of full mesh networks requires a significant amount of maintenance and expertise to manage.

> **Exam tip**
>
> Do not confuse the similarities between a mesh network and a peer-to-peer network; mesh networks can include the client–server model.

Check your understanding

10 Explain what a DNS does.

11 Explain **two** advantages of cloud computing.

12 Describe **one** advantage and one disadvantage of a star network.

Answers on p. 99

1.3.2 Wired and wireless networks, protocols and layers

In order for data to be transmitted on a network, the format of the data and the way the data is transmitted has to conform to an agreed set of rules or **protocols**.

Modes of connection

Wired	typically used in fixed sites such as offices and schools
	Ethernet protocols are used to transmit data on wired networks
	Ethernet uses MAC addresses to determine which device to send data to and what to do if collisions occur

Wireless	used when users need to move around the site and access the network from various locations
	often used as a supplement to a fixed wired network
	Wi-Fi protocols govern the way data is transmitted on a wireless network
	Wi-Fi standards determine the frequency band (2.4 GHz or 5 GHz), transmission rates and what should happen if there is a collision
	Bluetooth is another wireless protocol used over short distances using ultra-high frequencies; it is very secure and does not require line of sight
	Bluetooth is used to connect personal devices, such as headphones, to a mobile phone, or to connect two personal devices together to share information

Encryption

It is easy to intercept wireless signals, so most wireless networks encrypt the data.

✦ For a secure wireless network, a password is required to connect.
✦ The key is used to scramble the data.
✦ Only devices with the correct password will be able to unscramble the data.

> **Encrypt** means to scramble data using an algorithm and a key, so that it cannot be understood without the key to decrypt it

IP and MAC addressing

Every device connected to a network is assigned an IP address. This address is used to locate the device on the network. The address can change every time a device re-connects to the local network. These addresses are provided by the router.

IPv4 addresses use a 32-bit number, which is broken down into four 8-bit sections each representing a number between 0 and 255. An IPv4 address is usually written in denary with a full stop between each section.

For example: **194.83.249.5**

There are just over 4 billion different IPv4 addresses.

IPv6 addresses use a 128-bit number, which is broken down into eight 16-bit sections. IPv6 addresses are written using a hexadecimal character to represent each set of 4 bits, and with each section separated by a colon.

For example: **2001:0db8:3c4d:0015:0000:1234:1a2f:1a21**

There are 340 trillion, trillion trillion different IPv6 addresses.

A **MAC address** is a unique number assigned to an NIC at the manufacturing stage and cannot be changed. A MAC address is made up of 48 bits, shown as six groups of two hexadecimal digits.

For example: **b8:09:8a:b8:57:17**

41

Standards

REVISED ●

Standards are sets of rules that ensure hardware and software will work on different systems. Some common software standards include HTML for creating websites, and the MP3 file format for encoding audio files. Without these standards we would only be able to use hardware and software made by the same manufacturer.

Common protocols

REVISED ●

Network protocols establish a set of rules that govern how data is transmitted between devices.

The following protocols are used by web browsers and email clients.

Hypertext Transfer Protocol (HTTP)	defines the rules to be followed by a web browser and a web server when requesting and supplying data
Hypertext Transfer Protocol Secure (HTTPS)	uses Secure Sockets Layer (SSL) to encrypt communications between a web browser and a web server to ensure that they are secure
File Transfer Protocol (FTP)	defines the rules for transferring files between a client and a server
Post Office Protocol (POP)	used by a client to retrieve emails from a mail server; the emails are downloaded to the device and then deleted from the server. It is more or less obsolete these days
Internet Message Access Protocol (IMAP)	allows multiple devices to have synchronised access to mail on a mail server; messages are read rather than downloaded and can be organised and flagged
Simple Mail Transfer Protocol (SMTP)	defines the rules for sending email messages from a client to a server, and then from server to server

The following protocols determine how data is transmitted over a WAN.

Transmission Control Protocol (TCP)	splits the data from applications into smaller data packets that can be sent across a network; each packet has a header and a payload
	the header contains the sequence number of the packet and a checksum for error checking
	the payload is the data
Internet Protocol (IP)	adds a header to each data packet including the source and destination IP addresses; this determines how the data is sent between networks
	IP addresses are added to identify the source and the destination
	the IP address is used to determine where to send the data

A checksum is a value calculated from the data, which is recalculated on receipt to check if the data has been altered.

Layers

REVISED ●

When data is sent by a client, the individual packets of data are wrapped in information to ensure the packet is transmitted successfully. This is called **encapsulation**.

Protocols are assigned to layers and the data passes through each layer in turn to prepare it for transmission.

When data is received, it passes through these layers in reverse order to recover the data.

Function of the layer	Relevant protocols
application layer; allows communications between clients and servers	HTTP/HTTPS
	FTP
	POP
	IMAP
	SMTP
transport layer; splits the data into packets	TCP
internet layer; adds the IP addresses of the sender and recipient	IP
network access layer; adds the MAC addresses of the sender and recipient, and converts the data into electrical signals	Ethernet
	Wi-Fi

Advantages of layers.
⊕ Breaks down complex problems into smaller more manageable parts.
⊕ Each layer is self-contained and can be developed or changed independently of the other layers, providing the input and output are compatible with those layers.
⊕ Different manufacturers or developers can work on different layers independently.
⊕ Identifying problems can be narrowed down to a specific layer.

Check your understanding

13 State **two** protocols used in the transmission of emails.

14 Explain why we use agreed standards for hardware.

Answers on p. 99

Exam checklist

In this chapter you learned about:

Networks and topologies
+ Types of network
+ Factors that affect the performance of networks
+ Client–server and peer-to-peer networks
+ Hardware needed to connect computers into a LAN
+ The internet as a worldwide collection of computer networks
+ Star and mesh network topologies

Wired and wireless networks
+ Modes of connection
+ Encryption
+ IP and MAC addressing
+ Standards
+ Common protocols
+ Layers

Now test yourself

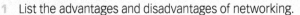 TESTED ○

1 List the advantages and disadvantages of networking.
2 List the factors that affect the speed of a network.
3 List the different types and topologies for a network and the advantages and disadvantages for each one.
4 List the hardware devices required to create a network.
5 List the key protocols and their use.

1 An estate agent has branches in several locations across the UK. Each branch has a connection to the internet and uses a number of peripheral devices such as printers and scanners.

   a) State **two** advantages of connecting devices in each branch with a LAN. [2]

   b) Explain **two** advantages of connecting the devices wirelessly. [2]

   c) Explain why connecting the branches together using a WAN would be useful to the business. [2]

   d) Explain what role a router will perform in this WAN. [2]

2 **a)** Describe the characteristics of a mesh topology. [2]

   b) Identify **three** reasons why an emergency service would choose a mesh topology. [3]

3 **a)** Describe how an IP address is used to access the internet. [2]

   b) Describe how a DNS is able to access a website using a URL. [3]

4 **a)** State **two** services provided by cloud computing. [2]

   b) Explain **three** advantages of cloud computing for a small accountancy business. [6]

5 Explain how layers are used when transmitting data on the internet. [4]

Answers on p. 103

1.4 Network security

Network security is about keeping networks, computers and the files, data and programs stored on them safe from attack, damage and unauthorised access.

1.4.1 Threats to computer systems and networks

There are a number of ways a computer network can be attacked.

Forms of attack

Malware are malicious programs that, once installed on a computer, are designed to cause damage or steal information. This table describes various types of malware.

Type of malware	What it does
virus	hidden inside, or attached to, another file or program
	virus code is run when the program is executed
	deletes or corrupts data and files
	can insert itself into other programs that can be passed on
	often passed on from files downloaded from a website or an infected storage device
worm	does not need to be hosted within another program
	self-replicating and causes the computer to run slowly or fail to respond
	creates backdoors so that hackers can take over the computer
	often spread by sending itself in emails to everyone in an address book
	can spread through computers in a network
Trojan	looks like legitimate software
	slows the computer and changes settings
	creates backdoors for hackers to access personal information using screenshots and key presses
ransomware	denies a user access to their system until a ransom is paid
	encrypts files and only decrypts them on payment of the ransom
spyware	often bundled with free software
	logs activity and keystrokes and sends these back to a criminal

Social engineering is a form of attack that tricks people into giving away important information or access details.

Form of attack	How it works
phishing	uses fake emails and websites to trick people into passing on important information
	often in the form of emails from a bank or supplier asking the user to click on a link
	the link is to a fake website that captures login, bank or other personal details
pretexting	often in the form of a phone call
	a scenario is created to persuade the user to divulge key information
	often the attacker will pretend to be from the police, bank or service supplier
shouldering	basically, looking over someone's shoulder to gather key information
	often used at an ATM or checkout to get a PIN or using recording equipment attached to the device

45

This table shows some other types of attack.

Form of attack	How it works
brute force	automated software attempts to crack a password by trying different combinations of numbers, letters and symbols until it finds the correct one
	commonly used and previously cracked passwords are tried first
denial of service (DoS)	servers are flooded with access requests in order to take down the server
	distributed denial of service (DDoS) attack uses compromised (zombie) machines infected with malware to create a botnet
	often used to extort a ransom or by hacktivists to attack an organisation they regard as unethical
pharming	redirects a user to a spoof website without their knowledge by modifying DNS entries
	can send lookup requests to a fake DNS or can infect a real DNS
	often redirects the user to the correct website after capturing login details so that the user is not aware of the attack

PIN stands for personal identification number; PINs are used with credit and debit cards.

Botnet is a collection of infected computers controlled by hackers.

Hacktivists are people who misuse computers for a socially or politically motivated reason.

Structured Query Language (SQL) is a language specifically designed for interacting with databases.

Data interception and theft: Data can be stolen using trojans, spyware or social engineering attacks.

Data is a valuable commodity.
+ Personal data can be used for identity theft or to access accounts.
+ Commercial data can be used to gain a competitive advantage.

Methods used for intercepting or accessing data include the following.

Packet sniffing: Intercepting data packets on a network, using software to manipulate a switch to send data to a device that analyses the data to read the contents. Wireless networks are particularly vulnerable since the signal can be accessed from up to 300 metres away, using a directional antenna.

Man in the middle: Accessing sensitive data by intercepting a device's connection to the internet often using fake Wi-Fi hotspots.

SQL injection: Many websites use SQL databases to store user details. SQL injection can bypass security by inputting valid SQL expressions instead of user details or searches. This causes a sequence of commands to be executed resulting in the release of sensitive data.

> **Check your understanding**
>
> 1 Explain what is meant by a *Trojan*.
> 2 Explain what is meant by *social engineering* to gain unauthorised access to a computer system.
> 3 Explain why data on a wireless network is more susceptible to interception.
>
> **Answers on p. 99**

1.4.2 Identifying and preventing vulnerabilities

Protecting networks and computer systems from threats

REVISED ●

Prevention method	Description
penetration testing	testers use hacking techniques in an attempt to break into a system to identify vulnerabilities that can be exploited in an attack
	assesses the ability of the organisation to respond to an attack and to recover any data that is lost or compromised
anti-malware software	designed to detect and remove malware from a system
	real-time scans of incoming data search for potential infections
	periodic scans of the whole system look for malicious software
	malicious software and infected files are quarantined to prevent them from running and to allow the user to clean or remove them
firewalls	software or hardware designed to prevent unauthorised access to a network
	inspect incoming and outgoing traffic to ensure that it meets the security criteria in the configured settings
	criteria include the MAC address of the computer sending the data, the type of data, and IP address filtering to prevent users accessing certain internet sites
network policies	sets of rules that all users of networks should follow. These can include password requirements, the use of removable devices and an acceptable use policy
	also detail factors concerning the type and frequency of backup, security measures to be used and user access rights
user access	network users are often split into groups with different user access rights
	access rights determine which files and software users can access
	confidential information can only be accessed by those with sufficient access rights
	most users may not be able to install software; this prevents them from installing malware
passwords	used to authenticate a user
	to make a password effective it should be kept securely and be difficult to work out
	use long passwords with a range of letters, numbers and symbols
	avoid the use of complete words or personal data such as names or dates
	use two factor authentication such as a separate code sent to the user at each login
	use biometric data instead of, or as well as, a password
encryption	data is encrypted so that if it is intercepted it is meaningless without the correct encryption key
	Wi-Fi networks should use secure encryption such as WPA2/3 to ensure data packets on the network cannot be intercepted and read
physical security	protecting hardware and software from physical actions such as theft or physical damage from intruders or natural disasters
	locked rooms prevent unauthorised access to equipment
	backups off-site to restore the system if data is lost or damaged

Biometric data uses unique biological characteristics such as retinal scans, fingerprints or facial recognition to verify the identity of an individual.

Wireless Access Protocol 2/3 (WPA2/3) is a type of encryption used to secure the vast majority of Wi-Fi networks. A WPA2/3 network provides unique encryption keys for each wireless client that connects to it.

Exam tip

With biometric data, the system does not store actual fingerprints or retina scans. Instead, it stores data calculated from these scans and compares what is stored to the scanned data.

47

Common prevention methods

Threat	Prevention methods
malware	install anti-virus and anti-spyware software
	install a firewall to prevent any data transmission by malware
	ensure that the operating system is up to date
	implement user access levels to prevent standard users from being able to install software
	only download programs from trusted websites
	educate users about the risks of opening emails and attachments from unknown sources
social engineering	educate users so that they are aware of the tactics of criminals and can guard against them
	ensure that network and security policies are followed
brute force attacks	use long passwords that include special characters
	use complex passphrases rather than single words
	use a password manager
	networks and websites can limit the number of login attempts allowed
	networks and websites can use two-step authentication
denial of service attacks	install a firewall to reject packets that originate from the same source or that have identical contents
	configure a firewall to restrict the number of packets that can be accepted within a particular time frame
SQL injection	use input validation to set password and username rules that don't permit characters that can be used in SQL injection attacks
	use input sanitisation to remove special characters and SQL command words from an input before processing it
data interception and theft	use strong encryption, especially on Wi-Fi networks; do not use unencrypted free public Wi-Fi networks
	use MAC address authentication on networks so that only known devices can connect
	ensure that websites are using HTTPS connections so that if data is intercepted it cannot be read
	install anti-malware software

Check your understanding

4 Explain what is meant by a *firewall*.

5 Describe **two** features that make passwords less susceptible to a brute force attack.

6 Describe how anti-malware software prevents infections by malicious software.

Answers on p. 99

Exam tip

It is not sufficient to install anti-malware software. The software must be used to scan for malware and be running constantly in the background to intercept malware.

Exam checklist

In this chapter you learned about:

Threats to computer systems and networks
+ Forms of attack
  + Malware
  + Social engineering, such as phishing, people as the 'weak point'
  + Brute force attacks
  + Denial of service attacks
  + Data interception and theft
  + The concept of SQL injection

Identifying and preventing vulnerabilities
+ Common prevention methods
  + Penetration testing
  + Anti-malware software
  + Firewalls
  + User access levels
  + Passwords
  + Encryption
  + Physical security

1 List **three** types of malware and describe how each one works.

2 List the main forms of attack and how to prevent them.

Exam-style questions

1 David has a wireless home network and is concerned about data and information being intercepted.

Describe **three** features that will minimise the possibility of data being intercepted. [6]

2 a) Explain how SQL injection can be used to gain unauthorised access to data in a database. [2]

b) Describe how SQL attacks can be prevented. [2]

3 A small business has asked a security expert to check on the security of their network.

a) Explain how the security expert might go about checking how secure a network is. [2]

b) The expert has recommended the business introduce a network policy.

i) Describe what is meant by a *network policy*. [2]

ii) Describe **three** features that might be found in a network policy. [6]

Answers on p. 104

1.5 System software

There are two main categories of software used on computers.
+ **System software** to control the hardware and provide an interface for the user.
+ **Application software** designed to perform specific tasks for the user.

1.5.1 Operating systems

An operating system (OS) is a collection of programs used in most computer devices – from mobile phones to large supercomputers – to tell the hardware what to do and allow the user to interact with the device.

Some well-known operating systems include:
+ Windows
+ macOS
+ Unix

+ Linux
+ iOS
+ Android.

The purpose and functionality of operating systems

REVISED ⬤

Operating systems provide:
+ a **user interface** to allow the user to interact with the system
+ an interface between the running program and the hardware
+ **peripheral management** to control devices using driver software
+ **memory management** to allocate memory to running programs
+ management of data transfers between memory locations, the CPU and secondary storage
+ **file management** to allow users to organise their work into folders
+ **user management** to control access to the system, files and software.

User interface

The user interface is where the user interacts with the computer. Most modern OSs provide a **graphical user interface (GUI)**. Most systems use a **Windows, Icons, Menus and Pointers (WIMP)** interface.

In a WIMP interface, applications are shown in windows with programs and files represented by icons. The menus allow the user to select features by moving a pointer controlled by a mouse or touch pad.
+ Using icons removes the need to learn commands for various actions.
+ It is particularly suited to touchscreen devices.

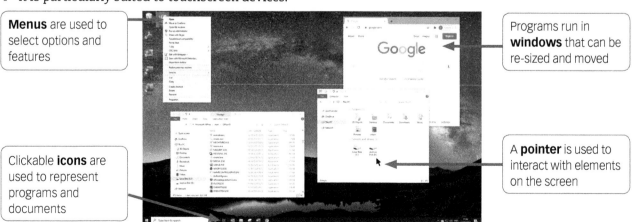

Menus are used to select options and features

Programs run in **windows** that can be re-sized and moved

Clickable **icons** are used to represent programs and documents

A **pointer** is used to interact with elements on the screen

Figure 1.5.1 A graphical user interface

(Google and the Google logo are registered trademarks of Google LLC, used with permission)

Before GUIs were developed, all users had to use a **command line interface (CLI)**, which meant typing all the commands via a keyboard. This included all the commands to load, copy, delete, move and print files. The commands had to be learned and used accurately.

Technicians still access and use the CLI to perform complex management actions. A sequence of commands can be grouped together, like a sort of computer program, in a **batch file** (Windows) or a **shell script** (Unix). The CLI is also used in for systems that require fast responses to commands such as systems used in power stations and particle accelerators.

Voice recognition technology is widely used in mobile phones and smart devices. Call centres often use voice recognition to deal with customer telephone enquiries.

Peripheral management

The operating system manages any peripheral devices used by the computer or device. A peripheral is any device that does not contribute to the core processing requirements for a computer.

+ Communication with the peripheral device is controlled by signals produced by the device drivers.
+ Device drivers are software provided by the manufacturer to communicate with the operating system.
+ Different OSs will require different device drivers.
+ Device drivers are regularly updated by the manufacturer to fix bugs or for minor modifications.
+ Device drivers handle data passed between the OS and the device, such as print data or data being sent to a USB memory device.
+ Data sent to a peripheral device is often stored temporarily in a buffer so that the device can deal with it at its own pace, for example print spooling.
+ The driver will wake up the device when it is needed and put it to sleep when it is not.

Memory management

Managing the available memory is one of the key tasks for the OS.

+ Several programs may be running at the same time. This is called **multitasking**.
  + The OS keeps the CPU as busy as possible to maximise the computer performance.
  + If the current program is waiting for data or loading data to secondary storage the OS will load another program to the CPU.
  + The CPU time is divided between processes by the OS allocating time to them based on priorities.
    + Users do not notice programs stopping and starting because it happens very quickly.
+ The memory manager allocates memory blocks to each program.
+ Programs can only access the memory allocated to them and cannot access memory allocated to other programs.
+ As programs complete and others start, the OS frees up the space and re-allocates it.

> **Exam tip**
>
> When a computer is multi-tasking it is still only running one program at a time. It switches between programs rapidly so it appears to the user to be working on more than one program at a time.

File management

The computer stores data and programs on secondary storage. The OS is responsible for storing and retrieving files.

✛ It provides facilities to manage files, for example save, delete, move, and so on.

✛ It manages the secondary storage dividing it up into identifiable areas so that the location of each file can be stored in an index.

✛ It creates file structures so that it is easier for the user to organise and locate files.

✛ It determines what to do with a file based on its type, for example execute a file or open a suitable application.

✛ On networks, the file manager is used to control who can access, write, delete or edit a file using file permissions.

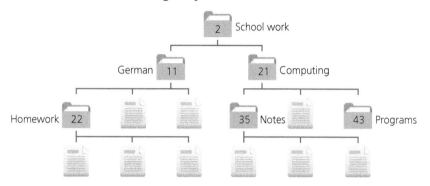

Figure 1.5.2 A hierarchical files system

A hierarchical files system is a directory that can expand as new files and folders are added to the disk. Each folder can be expanded with more files and folders.

User management

The OS manages who can access what.

✛ It allows users to be created or deleted.

✛ It will allocate permission for access to files, folders, applications and settings based on access rights.

✛ Access rights are often used to control who can install applications or change system passwords or control access to the internet.

Check your understanding

1 State **three** functions of an operating system.

2 Explain *peripheral management*.

3 Describe the role of user management in the OS of a computer.

Answers on p. 100

1.5.2 Utility software

Utility software is a collection of programs, often supplied with the OS, that support the OS by doing specific housekeeping tasks to maintain the computer system.

The purpose and functionality of utility software

REVISED ●

Utility software helps with configuring and managing the computer system. Some typical utility software include sencryption, defragmentation and data compression.

Encryption

Securing data on a computer from outside threats is important. Encryption scrambles the data so that it cannot be understood if it is accessed by an unauthorised user.

+ Encryption uses keys, or a pair of keys, with an algorithm that scrambles the plaintext into ciphertext. The same key and algorithm are required to unscramble the text.
+ Modern systems have built-in encryption utilities such as BitLocker or File Vault to encrypt files or even whole drives.
+ Data stored on removable devices is far more vulnerable to unauthorised access, and it is important for sensitive data to be encrypted using suitable software. The data can then only be accessed by someone using the same software and the correct key.

A simple encryption techniques is the Caesar cipher, which displaces characters by a fixed amount.

For example, displacing by five characters creates this lookup table:

Plaintext letter	A	B	C	D	E	F	G	H	I	J	K	L	M	N	O	P	Q	R	S	T	U	V	W	X	Y	Z
Ciphertext letter	V	W	X	Y	Z	A	B	C	D	E	F	G	H	I	J	K	L	M	N	O	P	Q	R	S	T	U

The plaintext message 'HELLO' becomes the ciphertext 'CZGGJ'.

The cipher text and the key 5 are required to decode the message.

Defragmentation

When data is saved to a hard disk drive the OS looks for available space. If the space available is not large enough to store the data in one place it is split into blocks and saved in several locations. This is called fragmentation.

+ Over time, as data is saved and removed, many larger files will be scattered across the drive and stored in multiple locations.
+ Since the read/write heads have to move between these fragments to read a file, it makes access times considerably slower.
+ Since SSDs do not have moving heads or rotating disks, there is no need to defragment a SSD.

Defragmentation organises and moves the separate parts of the data files so that they are stored together and can be accessed much more quickly.

Small blocks of free space are also grouped together to provide continuous reading from the HDD head. This also allows grouped free space of memory to be allocated to future data.

Fragmented data

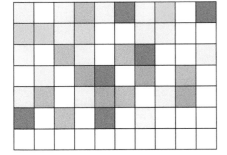

Defragmented data

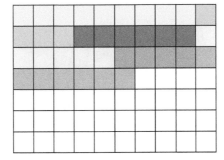

Figure 1.5.3 The process of defragmentation

53

Data compression

Data compression uses algorithms to reduce the size of a file.

Compressed files can be transmitted much more quickly over the internet.

When emailing files there is often a limit on the size of an attachment so large files need to be compressed.

There are two types of compression, lossy and lossless:
+ Lossy compression removes some of the data to reduce the file size; the original file cannot be restored.
+ Lossless compression uses algorithms to look for patterns and repeated elements in a file and stores these in a dictionary with a reference so that the data can be restored.

Check your understanding

4   Explain what is meant by *encryption software*.

5   Explain what is meant by *lossless compression*.

Answers on p. 100

Exam checklist

In this chapter you learned about:

Operating systems
+ The purpose and functionality of operating systems

Utility software
+ The purpose and functionality of utility software
+ Utility system software: encryption, defragmentation and compression

Now test yourself   TESTED ◯

1   List the features of an operating system.

2   Explain what is meant by *multitasking* and how it works.

3   List **three** items of utility software and what each one does.

Exam-style questions

1   **a)**   Andrew has a computer with a GUI.
        i)   Explain what is meant by a GUI.   [2]
        ii) Describe **two** features of a GUI.   [4]
    b)   Andrew's son wants to use the same computer. Andrew sets up another user for his son.
        Explain how Andrew might use features of user management to ensure his own data and programs are kept secure.   [2]
    c)   Andrew sends a lot of photographs to publishers.
        i)   Explain why he might need to use compression software.   [2]
        ii) Explain what type of compression software he would use and why it is appropriate.   [2]

2   **a)**   Describe what is meant by *file management*.   [2]
    b)   State and describe **two** features of file management.   [4]
    c)   Identify **two** items of utility software and describe their purpose. [4]

3   **a)**   Explain the purpose of the operating system in a computer.   [2]
    b)   Identify and describe **three** features of an operating system.   [6]

Answers on p. 104

1.6 Ethical, legal, cultural and environmental impacts of digital technology

1.6.1 Ethical, legal, cultural and environmental impact

The widespread use of computer technology in all aspects of daily life has brought many benefits for the individual and society. Computer systems are involved in most human activities. Alongside these benefits, the widespread use of computer technology has also generated various problems, from computer crime to issues with the freedom and privacy of the individual.

Impacts of digital technology on wider society

Ethical issues

Ethics refer to what is right and wrong and how people should behave. Computer organisations such as the British Computer Society (BCS) have codes of conduct that prescribe suitable ethical behaviour for its members.

Legal issues

Legal issues are laws drawn up to govern activities and control computer crime such as:
+ unauthorised access to data and computer systems for the purpose of theft or damage
+ identity theft
+ software piracy
+ fraud
+ harassment, such as trolling.

Cultural issues

Culture refers to the ideas, behaviour, beliefs and values of a group of people. Cultural issues relate to how computers have impacted our lives, including:
+ the widespread use of 'disposable' digital devices and the environmental consequences
+ the ways in which people interact with each other, such as social media
+ changes in the workplace
+ replacing human roles in organisations
+ changing human roles within organisations
+ widespread data collection about individuals
+ access to entertainment and social interaction
+ workforce monitoring.

> **Exam tip**
>
> Don't confuse ethical and legal issues. Ethics are not the same as legalities – some things may be unethical while not being illegal. A good legal system will be based on an ethical approach.

> **Trolling** is the systematic posting of derogatory messages with the intent to upset an individual.

Environmental issues

The **negative environmental** impacts of widespread computer use include:
+ large global energy requirements to run computer systems and data centres
+ the use of rare and non-renewable metals and minerals
+ computer components made from toxic materials that are a hazard to the environment and to human health if not disposed of properly.

The **positive environmental** impacts of widespread computer use include:
+ homeworking reduces the need to travel, which reduces CO_2 emissions
+ more on-screen documents means a reduction in the use of paper and other resources
+ computers enable scientific research that leads to more environmentally friendly technologies, such as electric cars, the design of solar panels, and so on.

Privacy issues

Using computers raises concerns about individual rights to privacy. Some of the positive (⊕) and negative (⊖) ways in which individuals are monitored are listed below.

Companies can monitor exactly what their workforce are doing on their computers.
⊕ It enables the employer to monitor the effectiveness of an employee.
⊕ It provides insight into working patterns.
⊕ It can reduce the risk of employees using the organisation's facilities for illegal or unacceptable purposes (for example, monitoring social media posts).
⊖ It is an intrusion into the lives of the employee.
⊖ It results in constant pressure to perform at work.

Use of closed-circuit television (CCTV) and facial recognition.
⊕ It is a form of security that can be used to solve crimes and keep us safe on the streets.
⊕ Live facial recognition can be used to identify and locate criminals.
⊖ It is a 'big brother' approach, constantly tracking what we do and where we go.
⊖ It is an invasion of privacy.

Automatic number plate recognition (ANPR).
⊕ The authorities can check that a car is taxed, insured and tested or reported as stolen or used in a crime.
⊖ Can be used to track the movements of an individual.

Websites can track a lot information about your internet activities: your location, your browser, your IP address, your operating system, what websites you have visited and what you have searched for.
⊕ This data might be used to provide insights to, for example, target advertising.
⊕ Can be used to track fraudulent or other criminal behaviour.
⊖ Such constant tracking is an intrusion into an individual's right to privacy.

Mobile phone companies are able to track an individual's location from their mobile phone, even if they are not using it. Mobile phone call records are also stored and can be accessed by law enforcement agencies if requested.
⊕ It is useful for finding friends.
⊕ It can provide valuable evidence for the police.
⊖ When we take a picture, the location and time are recorded tracking our activities.
⊖ There are apps that track our location at all times.

Social media activity is constantly monitored and many of us use social media to keep in touch with friends.

⊕ You can share recent activities to keep people up to date with what you like and what you are doing.

⊖ Trolling and cyber bullying are attempts to cause someone distress by posting insulting or threatening messages and can be very unpleasant.

⊖ Unguarded comments or inappropriate images posted on social media are available to a wide audience and may be seen by family, friends, work colleagues or employers.

⊖ With the wrong privacy settings, social media activity is available for anyone to see.

Censorship

Censorship is the deliberate suppression of material by an organisation or government. This may include:

✚ material considered to be socially unacceptable

✚ information that the organisation or government regards as dangerous

✚ access to websites; these are controlled by blacklists, which keep a record of unacceptable websites and monitor web pages to see if some or all of the content should be blocked.

The extent to which the internet is censored varies. At a local level, schools may filter content to protect students from unsuitable content. At a national level, some countries impose very strict filtering of content in order to prevent the population from debating political or cultural issues that its government does not approve of.

The debate is about where to draw the line between protecting the public and infringing their rights to free speech and access to information.

Check your understanding

1 Identify **three** ways computers impact on retail activities.

2 Describe **one** positive aspect of mobile phone tracking.

3 Explain **one** positive aspect of computer use to monitor people in public places using facial recognition.

Answers on p. 100

> **Exam tip**
>
> When answering a question, make sure you consider the viewpoint identified in the question. For example, the question may ask for positives from an employer's point of view.

Legislation relevant to computer science

REVISED ●

The Data Protection Act 2018

Computers hold vast amounts of data and it is important that this data is collected, stored and processed in ways that protect the individual. Every organisation holding personal data – apart from those with specific exemptions – must register with the Information Commissioner's Office and disclose what data they are holding, why they are collecting it and how it will be used.

Exemptions are granted to specific sectors including national security, scientific research, financial services and the Home Office.

The act sets out seven key principles that should be central to processing personal data.

1 Lawfulness, fairness and transparency

There must be valid reasons for collecting and using personal data.

It must be necessary for the stated purpose – if it can be achieved without collecting data then it is not lawful. Lawful bases for collecting data are:

+ consent from the data subject
+ for the purposes of fulfilling a contract
+ in order to comply with the law
+ it is in the interest of the individual, for example to protect their wellbeing
+ it is in the public interest
+ there is a legitimate interest in the data subject.

2 Purpose limitation

The purpose for processing the data must be clear from the start and it cannot be used for any other purpose not compatible with the original one.

3 Data minimisation

Data being processed must be adequate, relevant and limited to what is necessary.

4 Accuracy

All reasonable steps must be taken to ensure the personal data held is correct and not misleading and it must be kept up to date. If any data is incorrect or misleading, it must be corrected or erased as soon as possible.

5 Storage limitation

Data must not be kept for longer than necessary.

6 Security

There must be adequate security measures in place to protect the data held.

7 Accountability

The data holder must take responsibility for how the data is used and for compliance with the other principles of the act.

The Computer Misuse Act 1990

This act covers hacking and distributing malware. Under the act it is a criminal offence to make any unauthorised access to computer material:

+ with intent to commit further offences, such as blackmail; this provision refers to unauthorised access (commonly called hacking)
+ with the intent to modify the computer material; this provision refers to anything that impairs the performance of a computer system, such as the distribution of viruses.

Copyright, Designs and Patents Act 1988

This act protects the intellectual property of an individual or organisation.

The act makes it illegal to copy, modify or distribute software or other intellectual property (including music and video).

Software licences

Most commercial software will come with a licence agreement allowing the user to install software on a device. With proprietary software a licence will be required for each device the software is installed on.

Proprietary software is written by organisations trying to make a profit.

Open-source software uses a community of developers.

> **Exam tip**
>
> We often hear people say that using illegal copies of software or music is a victimless crime. Consider the large number of people and businesses involved in the supply of music and software beyond wealthy corporations, whose employees and their livelihoods are affected by those who bypass copyright laws.

> **Exam tip**
>
> There are no 'typical' users for open-source or proprietary software – many large organisations such as Amazon rely on open-source software because they have the in-house expertise to manage it effectively. A small business might choose proprietary software because they rely on a piece of software but lack the expertise to deal with problems or understand the community support available.

Open-source software	Proprietary software
access to the source code	no access to source code
may be free of charge	almost always some cost involved
users can modify the software	user cannot modify the software
can be installed on as many computers as necessary	extra licences must normally be obtained before installing on another computer
no one is responsible for any problems with the software	full support from the software developer
usually only community support	commercial and community support available

Creative Commons is an organisation that issues licences allowing a user to modify or distribute parts of the software under certain conditions. It is also known as 'some rights reserved'.

Typically, the authors might insist that the software is only used without payment in a non-commercial setting or that any use of the software includes statements that attribute the software to the original developers.

Check your understanding

4   State which law makes it illegal to distribute a virus.

5   Explain what is meant by *data minimisation* in the Data Protection Act.

6   Describe what is meant by *Creative Commons*.

Answers on p. 100

Exam checklist

Ethical, legal, cultural and environmental impact
+   Impacts of digital technology on wider society
    +   Ethical issues
    +   Legal issues
    +   Cultural issues
    +   Environmental issues
    +   Privacy issues
+   Legislation relevant to computer science
    +   Data Protection Act
    +   Computer Misuse Act
    +   Copyright, Designs and Patents Act
    +   Software licencing

Now test yourself

TESTED

1   State the **seven** key principles of the Data Protection Act 2018.

2   List **two** other acts and their purpose.

3   List the differences between *open source* and *proprietary* software.

Exam-style questions

1   Karen runs a small business with four employees, each with their own computer workstation connected to the internet.

a)   Karen is thinking about using open-source software. Discuss the issues she needs to consider before making a decision.   [4]

b)   Karen is concerned about staff using the internet for personal use while at work. Explain why she might have concerns about this.   [4]

2   Discuss the environmental impact of widespread computer use.   [8]

Answers on p. 105

Exam tip

If an exam question says 'discuss', you should look at more than one aspect of the topic, for example look at positive and negative aspects.

2.1 Algorithms

Computers are only able to solve a problem if they are given the right set of instructions by humans. An **algorithm** is a step-by-step set of instructions to solve a problem.

2.1.1 Computational thinking

Writing accurate algorithms that describe a solution to a problem is often quite complex. **Computational thinking** is an approach that uses three key principles that help us to write effective algorithms.

Principles of computational thinking

REVISED

Decomposition means breaking a complex problem down into smaller, more manageable parts.
+ Dealing with each small part of the problem is much simpler than trying to deal with a complex problem.
+ Breaking the problem down allows us to work on each sub-problem individually then combine those individual solutions into a solution for the whole problem.
+ For very large problems, a team of programmers can work on individual parts of the problem.

Abstraction involves taking a real-life situation and creating a model of it so that it can be analysed.
+ Removing or hiding unnecessary detail means the programmer can focus on the important aspects of the problem.

Algorithmic thinking is a method for defining the problem in a series of steps to be carried out in order to solve the problem.
+ Often, algorithms can be the basis for solutions to similar problems and looking for patterns can identify existing solutions to similar problems that can be adapted.

Check your understanding

1 Explain what is meant by *abstraction*.
2 Explain what is meant by *decomposition* of a problem.

Answers on p. 100

2.1.2 Designing, creating and refining algorithms

An algorithm must be precise enough to define a problem accurately and should include all the necessary steps in the process. It should be clear what instructions need to be followed, and what and when decisions need to be made.

Inputs, processes and outputs

Input refers to the data given to the algorithm. This may be user input typed in at the keyboard, automatically collected by sensors or provided from a data file.

Output is the data given back by the algorithm to the user. This may be a message on screen, printed output, sounds, images or data stored to a data file.

Processing is how the data supplied is manipulated by the algorithm to provide the desired output.

Figure 2.1.1 input–process–output

Structure diagrams

A structure diagram is a visual representation of a top-down design that is used to decompose a problem. At each step the next level is developed by deciding what is required to complete that step. When decomposing an online retail system we might identify four sub-problems, as shown in Figure 2.1.2.

Figure 2.1.2 Two-level structure diagram

This structure can be expanded further by deciding what is required for the sales module.

Figure 2.1.3 Three-level structure diagram

The process is repeated for all the steps at this level as necessary.

The process continues by adding levels below these where we need to clarify further what is required. This process carries on until each step is clearly defined.

Create, interpret, correct, complete and refine algorithms

Flowcharts

The inputs, processes, outputs and decisions required for an algorithm can be represented graphically using a flowchart.

A flowchart may use any of the following symbols:

⟶	Line	An arrow represents control passing between the connected shapes.	
▭	Process	This shape represents something being performed or done.	
▯▯▯	Subroutine	This shape represents a subroutine call that will relate to separate, non-linked flowchart.	
▱	Input/ output	This shape represents the input or output of something into or out of the flowchart.	
◇	Decision	This shape represents a decision (Yes/No or True/False) that results in two lines representing the different possible outcomes.	
⬭	Terminal	This shape represents the 'Start' and 'End' of the process.	

Figure 2.1.4 Flow chart symbols

- ✦ All flowcharts start (and often end) with the terminal shape.
- ✦ Inputs and outputs are represented by a parallelogram.
- ✦ Decisions are represented by a rhombus shape with two outgoing paths, Yes/No or True/False.
- ✦ Loops are represented using one or more rhombus shapes.
- ✦ Processes are represented by rectangles.
- ✦ The symbol to call a subroutine is the rectangle with two vertical lines.

For the retail system we could define a reordering system for when stock is low using the following flowchart:

> Subroutines are separate pieces of code that can be called from within a program. After the subroutine has completed its task, control returns to the main program.

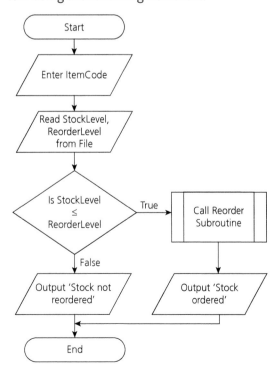

Figure 2.1.5 Flowchart for retail reordering system

Pseudocode

Pseudocode is an alternative way of presenting an algorithm using a structured form of English. The pseudocode algorithm will show the structure of the solution without using the formal syntax of a high-level language.

The ordering system represented by the flowchart could be written in pseudocode:

```
01 INPUT ItemCode
02 READ StockLevel, ReorderLevel From File
03 IF StockLevel <= ReorderLevel THEN
04    Call ReOrder()
05    PRINT "Stock ordered"
06 ELSE
07    PRINT "Stock not reordered"
08 END IF
```

Syntax refers to the formal structure used when writing a program, and includes the spelling of key words and the punctuation and grammar required; computers only understand commands if they are typed precisely.

Identify common errors and trace tables

A trace table is a method for following through an algorithm to identify any errors.

The contents of each variable is shown after each line of the algorithm has been completed.

By manually tracing the algorithm for a number of values we can identify if it works as expected or where any errors occur.

For the reorder system above, we can test the algorithm for different items and stock levels.

Exam tip

Pseudocode is not strictly defined and variations on the exact words used are often acceptable. Unless you are told to use a specific style, such as the OCR Reference Language, any reasonable format will be acceptable as long as the steps to be taken are clear.

In this example, item 009 has a current stock level of 8 and a reorder level of 3.

Line	itemCode	StockLevel	ReorderLevel	Output	Comments
01: INPUT ItemCode	009				Item code 009 entered by user
02 : READ StockLevel, ReorderLevel From File	009	8	3		Values read in from external file
03: IF StockLevel <= ReorderLevel THEN	009	8	3		8 is NOT smaller than or equal to 3, so line 7 executed next
07: PRINT "Stock not reordered"	009	8	3	'Stock not reordered'	Correct output printed

We would repeat the trace for a range of values, including borderline and low stock levels, such as 3 and 1.

Check your understanding

Exam tip

While some values are input on one line and do not change, the value of the variable at each stage of the process should be shown.

3 This algorithm is designed to decide what bus fare rate to charge. Complete the trace table for the input value 7.

```
01  input age
02  if age < 5 then
03      fare = 'Free'
04  elseif age < 16 then
05      fare = 'Half fare'
06  else
07      fare = 'Full fare'
08  print(fare)
09  endif
```

Line	age	fare	Output	Comment

4 The following algorithm is designed to check if someone can ride a roller coaster. To ride they should be at least 1.5m tall and at least 11 years old.

```
01   input height
02   intup age
03   if height >= 1.5 and age >= 11 then
04     print('You can ride')
05   else
06     if height > 1.5 then
07         print('Sorry not tall enough')
08     endif
09     if age < 11
10         print('Sorry not old enough')
11     endif
12   endif
```

a) There are **two** syntax errors in the code.
   Identify the lines and write the corrected code for each of these.
b) There is also **one** logic error.
   Identify the line and write the corrected code.

Answers on p. 100

2.1.3 Searching and sorting algorithms

Standard searching algorithms

A search algorithm should be able to check a list of items and locate an item or report that the item is not in the list.

Linear search

A linear search looks at each item in turn until it finds the target item or reaches the end of the list. If it reaches the end of the list without finding the target item, it reports that the item has not been found.

> **Exam tip**
>
> You are not expected to remember the searching and sorting algorithms in pseudocode but you are expected to know how they work.

> **Worked example**
>
> | Position | 0 | 1 | 2 | 3 | 4 |
> |----------|-----|------|------|------|-----------|
> | Item | Banana | Grape | Pear | Apple | Strawberry |
> | | ↑ | ↑ | ↑ | ↑ | |
>
> When searching for 'Apple' in this list it looks at each position in turn until it finds Apple.
>
> It will return that Apple was found at position 3.
>
> It will have taken four steps to find the item.

Binary search

A binary search locates an item by continuously splitting the list in half and checking if the mid-point is the value being searched for. If it is not, it discards the half that does not contain the item. It requires a list to be sorted in order to do this.

If it reaches a list with just one item that is not the target item, it reports that the item as not found.

When splitting the list into two halves, if there is no mid-point, we take the value to the left of the mid-point. (Either side could be taken provided we are consistent about this.)

> **Worked example**
>
> To search for B in this list:
>
> | Position | 0 | 1 | 2 | 3 | 4 | 5 | 6 | 7 |
> |----------|---|---|---|---|---|---|---|---|
> | Letter | A | B | C | D | E | F | G | H |
>
> There are eight items. There is no exact mid-point, so we choose D, to the left of the mid-point.
>
> | Position | 0 | 1 | 2 | 3 | 4 | 5 | 6 | 7 |
> |----------|---|---|---|---|---|---|---|---|
> | Letter | A | B | C | D | E | F | G | H |
>
> mid-point
>
> D is not the item being searched for, and B is before D alphabetically, so we discard the upper half (right-hand side), including the mid-point.
>
> | Position | 0 | 1 | 2 |
> |----------|---|---|---|
> | Letter | A | B | C |
>
> mid-point
>
> There are three items. The mid-point is B.
>
> The algorithm has located B at position 1.

Search method	Advantages	Disadvantages
linear	can search an unordered list	may be slow if the value is near the end of the list
		needs to search through the complete list to report if a value is not found
binary	usually much faster than a linear search. the number of items in the list halves after each iteration. to find a value in 1 million numbers takes just 21 iterations, a linear search may need 1 million iterations	the list must be ordered

Standard sorting algorithms

A sorting algorithm is used to put a list of values in order.

Bubble sort

+ Start at the beginning of the list and compare the first two items.
+ If they are in order, leave them.
+ If they are not in order, swap them over and record that a swap has taken place by setting a flag to True.
+ Now look at items 2 and 3, then 3 and 4, until the end of the list is reached.
+ If a swap has been made, start again at the beginning.
+ Repeat this process until no swaps are made on a complete pass through the list.

> A flag is a Boolean variable used to signal if something has happened; in the case of sorting, if a swap has taken place, the flag is set to True. The flag is used to decide if the list was in order and no swaps have taken place or not in order and some swaps have taken place.

Worked example

For the list D A C B E:

D	A	C	B	E	D and A are not in order so we swap them and set a swaps flag to True.
A	D	C	B	E	D and C are not in order so we swap and the swaps flag is True.
A	C	D	B	E	D and B are not in order so we swap and the swaps flag is True.
A	C	B	D	E	D and E are in order so no action.
A	C	B	D	E	Pass completed. The swaps flag is True so we set it to False and start again.
A	C	B	D	E	A and C are in order no action.
A	C	B	D	E	C and B are not in order so we swap and set the swaps flag to True.
A	B	C	D	E	C and D are in order so no action.
A	B	C	D	E	D and E are in order so no action.
A	B	C	D	E	Pass completed. The swaps flag is True so we set it to False and start again.

Since the data is now in order the next pass will complete without any swaps and the swaps flag will be False at the end of the pass. The algorithm stops.

Insertion sort

The insertion sort takes each item from an unsorted list and places it into a sorted list in the correct position.
+ It does this by splitting the list into a sorted side and an unsorted side.
+ Because a list with a single item must be a sorted list, initially the sorted side contains just the first item in the list.

Worked example

For the unsorted list:

Unsorted
D A C F B E H G

Split into a sorted list with just the first element of the list, and an unsorted list with the remaining elements.

Sorted	Unsorted
D	A C F B E H G

Take the first item in the unsorted list and insert into the correct place in the sorted list.

Sorted	Unsorted
A D	C F B E H G

C is now the first item in the unsorted list, so we insert it into the sorted list between A and D.

Sorted	Unsorted
A C D	F B E H G

Repeat the process taking the first item from the unsorted list and inserting it into the sorted list.

Sorted	Unsorted
A C D F	B E H G

Sorted	Unsorted
A B C D F	E H G

Sorted	Unsorted
A B C D E F	H G

Sorted	Unsorted
A B C D E F H	G

Sorted
A B C D E F G H

Merge sort

Consider how two sorted lists can be merged into a single sorted list.
+ Compare the first two items in each list.
+ Remove the one that comes first and add it to a new list.
+ Repeat this process until one list is empty.
+ Add the remaining items in the non-empty list to the new list.

Worked example

For the two lists:

List 1	List 2
3, 5	4, 8, 9, 11

Compare 3 and 4. 3 is the smallest so it is removed and placed in the new list.

New list
3

List 1	List 2
5	4, 8, 9, 11

Now we compare 5 and 4. 4 is the smallest so we remove it and place it in the new list.

New list
3, 4

List 1	List 2
5	8, 9, 11

Now we compare 5 and 8. 5 is the smallest so we remove it and place it in the new list.

New list
3, 4, 5

List 1	List 2
	8, 9, 11

List 1 is now empty so we append the contents of list 2 onto the new list.

New list
3, 4, 5, 8, 9, 11

If we are starting from an unordered list we create a set of ordered lists by breaking the unordered list down into lists containing just one item.

We merge each pair of lists in turn into two item lists, then four item lists and so on, until we have a single sorted list.

Worked example

For the list:

DACFBEHG

Split into single item lists:

D   A   C   F   B   E   H   G

Now we merge each pair into two item lists:

AD   CF   BE   GH

Merge in pairs again:

ACDF   BEGH

Merge the list until we have a single sorted list:

ABCDEFGH

Sort	Advantages	Disadvantages
bubble	easy to program	takes many steps to complete the process, even for a small list it is inefficient and not suited to large lists
insertion	easy to program good for small lists doesn't use a lot of memory compared to the merge sort quick to check if a list is already sorted	not very efficient with large lists
merge	more efficient than a bubble sort and more efficient than an insertion sort for large lists takes the same time for a list regardless of how unordered it is	slow for small lists takes up a lot of memory because it creates so many lists

Check your understanding

5 Show the process for sorting the list C D B A using:
   a) bubble sort   b) merge sort   c) insertion sort.
6 Show the process for finding F in the list A B C D E F G using a binary search.

Answers on p. 100

Exam tip

You may be asked to complete a search or a sort for a given data set. Show the steps and annotate the process to explain how you have completed the task.

Exam checklist

In this chapter you learned about:

Computational thinking
+ Principles of computational thinking
   + Decomposition
   + Abstraction
   + Algorithmic thinking

Designing, creating and refining algorithms
+ Identifying the inputs, processes and outputs for a problem

+ Structure diagrams
+ Creating, interpreting, correcting, completing and refining algorithms
+ Identifying common errors
+ Trace tables

Searching and sorting algorithms
+ Standard searching algorithms
+ Standard sorting algorithms

Now test yourself

TESTED ◯

1 List the **three** key principles of computational thinking and their descriptions.
2 Outline how a linear search and a binary search work and the major differences between them.
3 Outline how bubble, insertion and merge sorts work.

Exam-style questions

1 Draw a flowchart to describe the following process.   [6]
   + Enter a number between 1 and 10 inclusive.
   + Reject values not in range and request the input again.
   + If it is a valid input calculate the square of the number.
   + Output the value and its square.

2 Write a pseudocode algorithm to describe a program that asks a user to input five numbers.

   The program will output the average of those five numbers.   [6]

3 a) For the list of plants:
   ivy, broom, poppy, fern, privet, lilac, dogwood, rose
   show the steps for a merge sort to put the list into ascending alphabetical order.   [4]

   b) Explain why a merge sort might be problematic for a set of data with several thousand items in it.   [2]

4 a) For the list of animals:
   cat, dog, frog, goat, horse, kangaroo, lion, monkey, parrot
   show the steps in a binary search to locate **lion**.   [3]

   b) State how many steps would it take to locate **lion** using a linear search.   [1]

   c) Explain when you would have to use a linear search to locate an item in a list.   [2]

   Answers on p. 106

2.2 Programming fundamentals

2.2.1 Programming fundamentals

Paper 2 requires knowledge and understanding of programming. Complete as much practical programming practice as possible in a high-level language such as Python, Visual Basic or C#.

All questions in the examination will be in the **OCR Reference Language**. However, your answers can be given in any high-level language of your choice.

Variables, constants and assignments

Variables are used in a computer program to store a single piece of data.
+ The contents of a variable may change during the running of a program.
+ When a variable is first defined, a small area of computer memory is allocated to store the data assigned to the variable.
+ An identifier is used as a label to refer to this area in memory.
+ Identifiers are case sensitive so Score and score are treated as different variables.
+ Identifiers can be almost anything, but must not contain a space, start with a number, or be a reserved word (a word that means something in the programming language such as print).

Constants are used to store data that has a fixed value.
+ Like a variable, a constant has an area of memory allocated and an identifier.
+ Unlike a variable, the value stored by the constant cannot change when the program is run.

Assignment means to give a variable or a constant a value.

The identifier always goes on the left and the assigned value on the right after the assignment symbol, often = (some languages use := or other symbols).

For example, to assign the sum of variables num1 and num2 to the variable total: `total = num1 + num2`

> **Common mistake**
>
> It is a common mistake to see a constant described as a variable that does not change. Variables and constants have many similarities but they are not the same.

Sequence, selection and iteration to control the flow of a program

There are three basic constructs used to create a computer program: sequence, selection (sometimes referred to as a decision) and iteration (often called a loop).

Sequence

Execute the statements one after the other.

> **Worked example**
>
> ```
> a = 10
> b = 5
> c = a * b
> print(c)
> ```

Selection

The path through the program is decided by looking at a condition.

Depending on the outcome of that condition one of two or more paths is followed.

Worked example

```
if temp < 20 then
    turn on heater
else
    turn off heater
endif
```

Iteration

To repeat a process based on a condition.

The condition can be a fixed number of times, a **count-controlled loop**.

Worked example

```
for k = 1 to 12
    print(k, "times 5 is ", k*5)
next k
```

The condition can be based on a condition being met, a **condition-controlled loop**.

While a condition is true, a **WHILE loop** is used:

Worked example

```
count = 0
while count < 12
    count = count + 1
    print(count, "times 5 is ", count*5)
endwhile
```

Until a condition is true, a **DO WHILE loop** (sometimes referred to as a DO UNTIL) is used:

Worked example

```
count = 0
do
    count = count + 1
    print(count, "times 5 is ", count*5)
until count == 12
```

Exam tip

Examiners will sometimes set questions based on incorrectly formed loops for you to correct. Look for infinite loops where the condition is never going to be met, or loops where the condition is not able to produce the expected result.

A WHILE loop checks the condition before the code section is executed.
+ A WHILE loop may not be executed at all if the condition returns false.

A DO WHILE loop checks the condition after the code section has been executed.
+ A DO WHILE loop will always execute at least once.

The common arithmetic operators

REVISED ○

Arithmetic operators are used to carry out basic mathematical operations on numeric values in a computer program. The common operators are:

Operator	Name	Example	Example
+	addition	`ans = num1 + num2`	`num1 = 2, num2 = 5` `ans = 2 + 5 = 7`
-	subtraction	`ans = num1 - num2`	`num1 = 9, num2 = 4` `ans = 9 - 4 = 5`
*	multiplication	`ans = num1 * num2`	`num1 = 2, num2 = 4` `ans = 2 * 4 = 8`
/	division	`ans  = num1/num2`	`num1 = 20, num2 = 5` `ans = 20 / 5 = 4`

MOD	modulus	`r = num1 MOD num2`	Returns the remainder after dividing `num1` by `num2`
			
			`num1 = 14, num2 = 3`
			
			`14/3 = 4 remainder 2`
			
			`r = 14 MOD 3 = 2`

DIV	quotient	`q = num1 DIV num2`	Returns the whole number part after dividing `num1` by `num2`
			
			`num1 = 14, num2 = 3`
			
			`14/3 = 4 remainder 2`
			
			`r = 14 DIV 3 = 4`

^	exponent	`ans = num1^num2`	Raises `num1` to the power of the `num2`
			
			`num1 = 2, num2 = 3`
			
			`ans = 2^3 = 8     (2 * 2 * 2)`

Exam tip

When addition, subtraction, multiplication and exponent are applied to integers, the result is an integer but this is *not* the case for division. Dividing one integer by another may result in a real number.

Modulus and quotient are mathematical operations that only apply to positive integers and always return a positive integer or 0 (whole numbers).

Key point

The MOD operator can be used to decide if a number is an exact multiple of another number; if it is the result will be 0. This is useful for deciding if a number is odd or even, if the result of MOD 2 is 0 the number is even, if it is 1 then the number is odd.

The operator precedence is the same as in mathematics, BIDMAS.
1. Brackets
2. Indices
3. Division and Multiplication
4. Addition and Subtraction

(5 − 3) * (3 + 2)	brackets first gives 2 * 5 = 10
5 * 3 − 2	multiplication first gives 15 − 2 = 13
5 * (3 − 2)	brackets first gives 5 * 1 = 5

The common Boolean operators

REVISED ●

When we compare two values, the result is either True or False.

Operator	Name	Examples	Comment
==	equal to	8 == 8 (true) 8 == 7 (false)	some languages may use a single = sign; do not confuse this with assignment!
!=	not equal to	5 != 7 (true) 5 != (3 + 2) (false)	!= gives the opposite outcome to ==; some languages may use < >
<	less than	4 < 7 (true) 4 < 4 (false) 7 < 5 (false)	gives a False output if the values are equal
<=	less than or equal to	7 <= 12 (true) 7 <= 7 (true) 6 <= 3 (false)	gives a True output if the values are equal
>	greater than	5 > 1 (true) 7 > 7 (false) 3 > 5 (false)	gives a False output if the values are equal
>=	greater than or equal to	9 >= 5 (true) 9 >= 9 (true) 5 >= 8 (false)	gives a True output if the values are equal

Boolean operators AND, OR and NOT

The common Boolean operators can be used to evaluate multiple conditions.
+ AND requires both conditions to be True for the overall condition to return True.
+ OR requires one or both of the conditions to be True to return True.
+ NOT inverts the results from True to False or False to True.

> Boolean operators are named after the English mathematician George Boole. George Boole determined that logical decisions could all be reduced to True or False outcomes.

Variables	Condition	Comment	Value returned
a = 5, b = 7 c = 4, d = 2	(a > b) AND (c > d)	5 is not greater than 7 so False 4 is greater than 2 so True	False
a = 5, b = 7 c = 4, d = 2	(a != b) AND (c >= d)	5 is not the same as 7 so True 4 is greater than 2 so True	True
a = 5, b = 7 c = 4, d = 2	(a > b) OR (c > d)	5 is not greater than 7 so False 4 is greater than 2 so True	True
a = 5, b = 7	NOT(a > b)	5 is not greater than 7 so that is False (but NOT inverts the result)	True

These operators are also used extensively in conditional statements to make decisions.

73

```
username = input("enter your username ")
password = input("enter your password ")
if username == "admin" and password == "changeme123" then
    print ("Correct details. Logged in")
else:
    print ("Incorrect details")
endif
```

In this example, the AND keyword means that both conditions (the username and password both matching the correct ones) need to be True for the user to be logged in.

Check your understanding

1 Calculate the value assigned to the variable x if:
   a) x = (13 – 4) / 3
   b) x = 5 * 4 / 2
   c) x = 13 – 2 * 4
   d) x = 15 MOD 6
   e) x = 29 DIV (2 * 3)

2 What is returned by the following comparisons?
   a) 3 != 3
   b) 3 < 5
   c) 3 <= 3 AND 5 > 4
   d) 8 >= 6 OR 5 != 6
   e) 3 == 5 OR 5 <= 5

Answers on p. 101

2.2.2 Data types

Variables and constants are allocated space in memory.

Different data types require different amounts of space.

There are five main data types to consider.

Data type	Comments	Example
integer	whole numbers such as quantities	6, –3, 2112, 0
real (float)	numbers with a decimal part, such as prices	3.23, –1.05, 15.65
Boolean	can only take one of two values, True or False	True/False, 1/0
character	a single character from the character set	A, g, N, 5, £
string	a string of alphanumeric characters such as names or telephone numbers	Cat, M325Tgl, @4$&eR

Float is used to cast variables as real numbers in some programming languages. It is short for floating point, a term that describes how the point can be placed anywhere within the digits of the number. We use a decimal point in denary to split the number into whole and decimal parts, for example 35.312.

Strings and characters require quotation marks around the values assigned to distinguish them from variable names.

colour = "blue" assigns the value "blue" to the variable colour.

colour = blue will try to assign the value of the variable blue to the variable colour. If the variable blue does not exist it will result in an error in the program.

Casting is the process of converting from one data type to another.

This is only possible if the data can sensibly be converted. We can convert the string "123" to the number 123, but there is no sensible way to convert the string "Holiday" to a numeric value.

Keyword	Converts to ...	Examples	Comment
`str()`	string	`a = str(123)` `b = str(True)`	converts any other data type into a string
`int()`	integer	`c = int("123")` `d = int(87.0)`	converts real numbers to integers by removing the decimal part and returning the integer part (it does not round the number); strings that only contain numeric values can be cast as integers
`real()`	real	`e = real("112.9")` `f = real(46)`	integers and strings that only contain numeric values can be cast as real numbers; some languages use `float()` to cast
`bool()`	Boolean	`g = bool("True")`	some languages will cast integers 1 and 0 to be True and False

Check your understanding

3 State whether the following are real numbers, integers, characters, strings or Boolean data types.
   a) "35.6"
   b) 17
   c) True
   d) 3.14159
   e) Seventeen
   f) "@"
   g) "2&3R5"

Answers on p. 101

2.2.3 Additional programming techniques

The use of basic string manipulation

 REVISED

Function	Explanation	Example
length	returns the length of a string	`if text = "Computing is fun"` `text.length = 16`
substring	we can separate substrings by position or by start and length	`if text = "Computing is fun"` `text.substring (2,5) = "mputi"` `text.left(4) = "Comp"` `text.right(5) = "s fun"`
case	we can convert between upper and lower case using .upper and .lower	`If text1 = "Bridge"` `text.upper = "BRIDGE"` `text.lower = "bridge"`
ASCII conversion	to switch between a character and its ASCII value	`ASC("D") = 68` `CHR(68) = "D"`
concatenation	we can join two strings together by concatenating them with +	`text2 = "ginger"` `text3 = "cat"` `text4 = text2+text3`

The use of basic file handling operations

When a program ends, the data stored in the variables is lost. To keep data that is required again we can store it in text files.

Opening and closing a file

Before a text file can be used it needs to be opened. The OCR Reference Language uses the keyword `open()` to do this.

To open a file, the file name is passed as a parameter in brackets and assigned to a variable:

```
names = open("formlist.txt")
```

To close the file once it has been used, the OCR Reference Language uses the `close()` keyword.

```
names.close()
```

Reading from a file

To read a line of text from an open file the `.readLine()` keyword is used.

If it is used multiple times it will return the next line each time.

The `endOfFile()` keyword returns a Boolean True or False value to indicate whether the end of file has been reached. This can be used with a WHILE loop and the `readLine()` keyword to read lines of text until it reaches the end of the file.

Writing to a file

To write text to a file the keyword `.writeLine(x)` will add the string x to the end of the file.

Worked example

```
names = open("formlist.txt")
while NOT names.endOfFile()
   student = names.readLine()
   print(student)
endwhile
names.close()
```

Worked example

```
names = open("formlist.txt")
newdata = ""
while newdata != "stop"
   newdata = input("Enter a student name ")
   if newdata !="stop"
    names.writeLine(newdata)
   endif
endwhile
names.close()
```

The use of records to store data

A record is a data structure used within a database to store data by categories under key fields. To create a record we first need to set up the field names. For example, for an address book: FirstName, LastName, Telephone, Email

The data for each person is stored under these headings in a table.

A table must have a name to identify it; we shall call it 'tblNames'.

FirstName	LastName	Telephone	Email
Bill	Wilson	02222347593	bw@notreal.com
Graham	Mills	02121398741	graham@notreal.com
Imran	Mahmud	02231974522	imahmud@notreal.com
Sally	Jones	02231987342	sally@notreal.com

← Records

Fields

SQL to search for data

Structured Query Language (SQL) is a language used to access data stored in a database.

There are three important keywords.

SELECT	identifies the fields to be returned by the query; we can use * as a wildcard to return all data
FROM	identifies the database table(s) to use
WHERE	allows the programmer to include any criteria the data should match

Worked example

Using the table tblNames

```
SELECT FirstName, Email FROM tblNames
```

Will return the data:

Bill, bw@notreal.com

Graham, graham@notreal.com

Imran, imahmud@notreal.com

Sally, sally@notreal.com

Worked example

```
SELECT FirstName, Telephone
FROM tblNames
WHERE lastName = 'Mills'
```

Will return the data:

Graham, 02121398741

Worked example

```
SELECT *
FROM tblNames
WHERE firstName = 'Sally' OR lastName = 'Wilson'
```

Will return the data:

Bill, Wilson, 02222347593, bw@notreal.com

Sally, Jones, 02231987342, sally@notreal.com

One- and two-dimensional arrays

When solving problems with lots of variables, all of the same description, rather than create these individually we assign the values to an array.

An array:
+ holds a fixed number of elements; the size is defined when the array is created
+ can only hold data of the same type
+ uses a single identifier and an index.

One-dimensional arrays

To store five names we can create an array called **names**.

In OCR Reference Language:

```
array names[5]

names[0] = "Henry"

names[1] = "Alan"

names[2] = "Jane"

names[3] = "Li"

names[4] = "Umar"
```

0	1	2	3	4
Henry	Alan	Jane	Li	Umar

> **Key point**
>
> Computer scientists start counting at 0 so for 5 items the index values are 0 to 4.

Worked example

We can use a for loop to access the elements of a one-dimensional array:

```
for index = 0 to 4

    print(names[index])

next index
```

Two-dimensional arrays

Where there are two categories of information – for example, names and groups – we can use a two-dimensional array.

A two-dimensional array is accessed using two index numbers.

Two-dimensional arrays are often shown as tables with rows and columns.

For students in three groups of four, we might show the data like this array names[3,4].

	0	1	2
0	Henry	Ben	Li
1	Umar	Chen	Hannah
2	Abid	Mary	Keith
3	Jenny	Imran	Jane

> **Exam tip**
>
> The table is only a representation of a two-dimensional array and the data can be accessed either via [row, column] or [column, row]. In exam questions using 2D arrays represented by a table you will be told how to access the array.

If we access the table above using [row, column] then

```
names[1,2] = "Hannah"
```

To populate this array with names we would use nested for loops:

```
for i = 0 to 3
   for j = 0 to 2
     names[i,j] = input("Enter a name ")
   next j
 next i
```

How to use subprograms (procedures and functions) to produce structured code

REVISED ●

Apart from simple programs, most programs will consist of several modules, each performing a part of the task. Using subprograms (sometimes called subroutines) has several advantages including:

+ it reduces the overall size of the program by not repeating code in several places
+ it makes the code easier to understand and maintain
+ it saves time as they only need to be written and debugged in one place
+ it allows the reuse of code between programs, especially where pre-written and pre-tested subprograms can be used.

When we call a subprogram, control is passed from the main program to the subprogram.

Once the subprogram completes, it passes control back to the main program.

There are two main types of subprogram: procedures and functions.

Procedures and functions

+ Procedures and functions are defined outside the main body of the program.
+ They have their own identifiers so they can be called as often and as many times as necessary.
+ Data can be passed from the main program into the subprogram using a parameter.
+ Parameters are identified in brackets after the identifier for the subprogram.

Functions differ from procedures in one key way: a function returns a value back to the main program when it passes control back to it.

A procedure to print the area of a circle:

```
//procedure definition
   procedure area()
      radius = "Enter the radius of the circle")
      const pi = 3.14159
      print(pi * radius * radius)
   endprocedure
//call the subroutine
   area()
```

Notice the brackets after area when it is called are empty, but could have been used to pass a parameter. In this example the radius could have been passed if it was already known.

Worked example

```
//procedure definition
    procedure area(radius)
        const pi = 3.14159
        print(pi * radius * radius)
    endprocedure
//call the subroutine with the value 5, then with the
value 8
    area(5)
    area(8)
```

If we were to use a function to calculate the area of a circle, it would not print the value for the area but would pass it back to the main program to be used in further calculations or to be printed.

Worked example

```
//function definition
    function area(radius)
        const pi = 3.14159
        area = (pi * radius * radius)
        return area
    endfunction
//call the subroutine with the value 5
    new = area(5)
    print(new)
```

Random number generation

REVISED ○

One common built-in function in programming languages is the ability to generate random numbers.

Typically, an upper and lower limit are passed as parameters to generate a number within a range.

For example:

x = random(1,10) will generate an integer between 1 and 10.

y = random(-1.0, 5.0) will generate a real number between –1.0 and +5.0.

Check your understanding

4 If `text = "Revision"` and `name = "Frank"`, state the result returned by:
   a) `text.length`
   b) `text.substring(1,3)`
   c) `name.upper`
   d) `name+"'s "+text.lower`

5 The data table tblstaff, below, shows some details for employees of a business.

lastName	firstName	city	lengthEmployed	salary
Amaya	Camilla	Birmingham	3	32000
Cohen	Daniel	London	5	28000
Smith	Drew	Birmingham	1	19000
Holland	Sarah	London	7	45000
Hernandez	Jay	London	2	30000

State what is returned by the following SQL queries.

   a) `SELECT lastName`
      `FROM tblstaff`
      `WHERE city = 'London'`
   b) `SELECT city, lengthEmployed`
      `FROM tblstaff`
      `WHERE salary > 30000`
   c) `SELECT lastName`
      `FROM tblstaff`
      `WHERE lengthEmployed < 5 and salary > 30000`

6 In this array the data is accessed by `[row,column]` so `plant[1,2] = "Ivy"`.

Geranium	Rose	Violet	Tulip
Daffodil	Primrose	Ivy	Peoni
Clematis	Helibore	Wallflower	Poppy

   a) State what is returned by `plant[2,3]`.
   b) State the index of the array element for `"Violet"`.

Answers on p. 101

Exam checklist

In this chapter you learned about:

Programming fundamentals
+ The use of variables, constants and assignments
+ The use of sequence, selection and iteration to control the flow of a program
+ The common arithmetic operators
+ The common Boolean operators AND, OR and NOT

Data types

Additional programming techniques
+ The use of basic string manipulation
+ The use of basic file handling operations
+ The use of records to store data
+ The use of SQL to search for data
+ The use of one-dimensional and two-dimensional arrays
+ How to use subprograms (procedures and functions) to produce structured code
+ Random number generation

Now test yourself

TESTED ⬤

1 List the **three** programming constructs and an example of each one.
2 List the data types and an example of each one.
3 Show the structure of a typical SQL query and say what each part identifies.
4 List the benefits of subprograms.

Exam-style questions

1 Describe a variable and state how it differs from a constant. [3]

2 This program outputs a series of numbers:

```
value = 0

num = input("Enter a number ")

while value < num

    print(value, value*num)

    value = value + 1

endwhile
```

State what is output if the user enters the number 3. [3]

3 A one-dimensional array, values, with five elements contains five integers.

Write a pseudocode program to add together the numbers and output the total. [6]

4 The data table tblCities contains data about average temperature, hours of sun and rainfall in July.

city	country	rainfall	temp	hoursSun
London	UK	15	22	7
Rome	Italy	5	34	12
Oslo	Norway	23	19	6
Paris	France	8	28	10

State what is returned by the following queries.

a) SELECT city
   FROM tblCities
   WHERE hoursSun < 10 [2]

b) SELECT rainfall, temp
   FROM tblCities
   WHERE country = 'Norway' or
   country = 'UK' [2]

c) Write an SQL statement to return all the data about cities where the rainfall is less than 10. [3]

Answers on p. 106

2.3 Producing robust programs

It is not enough that a program works under ideal conditions; a program should be robust and work effectively under a range of conditions and with a range of users.

2.3.1 Defensive design

Defensive design is thinking about problems that could occur and building into the program design methods to deal with those anticipated problems.

Defensive design considerations

Anticipating misuse

A major source of problems will be unexpected or erroneous inputs. To minimise accidental errors where the user misunderstands what is required or deliberately attempts to break the system we can:

+ use meaningful prompts for each input
+ consider the combined effects of valid but atypical data
+ trap unexpected inputs
+ anticipate misuse and build in error-trapping to overcome this
+ authenticate the user.

Authenticating the user is establishing who is trying to access the system using:

+ **usernames and passwords** – probably the most common method for this; the username and password entered by the user are checked against the details held on the system
+ **electronic keys** – require the user to have sole access to a device such as a mobile phone. A text or email containing a one-time security code is sent to the device
+ **two-factor authentication** – uses a combination of two methods to authenticate a user, typically using electronic devices to send a code or request additional actions to authenticate a user who has logged in using a username and password
+ **biometrics** – uses electronic measurements relating to a biological characteristic such as a fingerprint, retina scan, facial recognition or voice recognition; banks are increasingly using voice profiles of customers to authenticate users phoning the bank.

Input validation

To trap unexpected or erroneous inputs the data input can be validated against a range of criteria, such as a presence check – a validation method that prevents a user from leaving a field blank.

Other criteria include:

+ type (for example, integer, string, real or Boolean)
+ range (for example, between 1 and 10)
+ format (for example, a date is in the dd/mm/yyyy format)
+ length (for example, more than eight characters in a password).

> **Exam tip**
>
> Validation can only check that the data is possible, for example that a date is in the correct format and within an acceptable range. It cannot check that the date entered is, for example, the correct birthdate for an individual.

Maintainability

Apart from the simplest programs, it is unlikely a program will be error-free in its first versions.

Over time, the requirements for a program may change and the program will require some modification.

Programs need to be well structured and documented to ensure that they are maintainable.

Subprograms

By splitting the program into a number of subprograms:
+ code repetition can be reduced
+ important processes can be modified in one place rather than trying to identify every occurrence.

Worked example

This table shows six prices all reduced by the same discount.

In example A, the code is copied, pasted and adjusted for each price. If we wanted to change the discount we would have to edit each calculation.

In example B, the prices are passed to the procedure. If we wish to apply a different discount we only have to change the value in one place. This means there is less chance of making a mistake and the code is not only easier to understand but is more maintainable.

Example A

```
price1 = 25 * 0.85
print("The discounted price is £", price1)
price2 = 50 * 0.85
print("The discounted price is £", price2)
price3 = 75 * 0.85
print("The discounted price is £", price3)
price4 = 120 * 0.85
print("The discounted price is £", price4)
price5= 70 * 0.85
print("The discounted price is £", price5)
price6 = 90 * 0.85
print("The discounted price is £", price6)
```

Example B

```
procedure calc(price)
    saleprice = price * 0.85
    print("The discounted prices is £",newprice)
endprocedure
calc(25)
calc(50)
calc(75)
calc(120)
calc(70)
calc(90)
```

Naming conventions

Using variable and subprogram names that describe their purpose makes it much easier for those who need to maintain the code to understand what each part does.

Indentation

Indentation clarifies the structure of a program. By indenting blocks of code within loops we can easily see what code belongs inside a block.

Worked example

This is the same program written without indentations and with indentations. In example B, it is clear what code is inside what loop making it easier to follow.

Example A

```
age = input("Enter your age:")
if age >= 17 then
print("Old enough to drive")
if age >= 18 then
print("and to vote.")
else
print("but not to vote.")
endif
else
print("Too young for both")
endif
```

Example B

```
age = input("Enter your age:")
if age >= 17 then
    print("Old enough to drive")
    if age >= 18 then
        print("and to vote.")
    else
        print("but not to vote.")
    endif
else
    print("Too young for both")
endif
```

Commenting

By adding comments to a program, the programmer can explain what each section of code does, making it easier to understand how the code works and carry out any maintenance on the program.

Worked example

```
function calcSalePrice(price, discount)
//function to return discounted price using original
price and percentage discount passed to it
    saleprice = price * (1-discount/100)
    return saleprice
endfunction
```

In this code, the comment provides a description of the function that tells the programmer what the function does and what data is expected.

My Revision Notes: OCR GCSE Computer Science

2.3.2 Testing

The purpose of testing

REVISED

Systematic testing of a program makes sure that it functions as expected and that it is robust. It is important that testing not only looks at how the program functions under normal circumstances but also looks at how well it functions in all circumstances. Testing should include destructive testing in an attempt to break the program. Only by showing that it is not easy to break the program can we be satisfied that it works.

> Destructive testing is actively trying to break the program to check if it is robust.

Types of testing

REVISED

Iterative testing

Sometimes referred to as 'white box testing', iterative testing is testing of the program at every stage in the development.

+ Programs are checked at modular level during development.
+ As each new module is added, the program is tested to check that no new errors have been introduced and that data from previous modules works with the new one.
+ Identifying faults in an individual module may be harder once modules are combined.

> Modules are the independent sections of a larger program. Modular programming breaks down a large task into a number of separate, independent tasks.

Final/terminal testing

Sometimes referred to as 'black box testing', final/terminal testing is testing to check if the whole system works as expected.

+ The modular detail is ignored at this stage of testing.
+ Final testing checks that the modules are correctly assembled into a working solution.
+ This stage of testing should also consider real data and real user inputs and actions.

Identify syntax and logic errors

REVISED

Syntax errors

Syntax errors occur when the rules of the language have been broken or used incorrectly.

For example:

+ variables not declared properly before use
+ incompatible data types
+ incorrect assignment, for example 3 + 4 = x instead of x = 3 + 4
+ use of reserved words for variables
+ variable names incorrect, for example spelling or formatting
+ instructions incorrectly spelled, for example pirnt instead of print.

> Syntax errors are mistakes in the use of the programming language rules that will prevent the program from running.

A syntax error will cause the program to stop running or not run in the first place because the translator cannot make sense of the instructions.

Logic errors

Logic errors occur during run-time and might produce unexpected or incorrect results.

For example:
+ division by zero will stop the program
+ programs may not complete because of loop conditions being incorrect
+ the memory is filled with data causing the program to crash
+ incorrect output.

The main causes of logic errors are:
+ conditions that cannot be met in conditional statements
+ divisors that can reach zero
+ incorrect algorithms (it doesn't do what it was meant to)
+ incorrect expressions (for example missing brackets or incorrect operators).

> **Logic errors** do not prevent the code from running but may cause the program to stop or crash or simply output incorrect results.

Selecting and using suitable test data   REVISED ●

To test a program effectively, it is necessary to identify suitable test data and expected outcomes.

Typically, a test plan is designed using a table.

Test data	Type of test data	Reason	Expected result	Actual result
should be actual data, not a description of the type of data	should indicate what type of data this is: normal, boundary, invalid or erroneous	should give the reason for using this test data and what it will check/show	what is *expected* to happen, either the output or that the data will be rejected or accepted	the *actual* result of the test

+ **Normal test data** is data of the correct type and range expected during normal use of the program. The data should be accepted and produce the desired result without causing errors.
+ **Boundary test data** is data that is of the correct type but sits right at the very edge of the acceptable range. This tests that the program works correctly with the full range of potential valid inputs. It should be accepted by the program and produce the desired result without causing errors.
+ **Invalid test data** is data that is of the correct type but outside the acceptable range. Invalid data should be rejected by the program.
+ **Erroneous test data** is data that is of the incorrect type and should be rejected by the program, for example a string input instead of a numeric one.

Testing should cover as many of the potential situations as possible including the full range of test data types.

> **Common mistake**
>
> It is a common mistake to simply identify the sort of data to be used rather than the actual value. Saying a number in the range 0 to 10 is *not* specific enough; an actual value, such as 7, should be included in the test plan.

Refining algorithms   REVISED ●

Refining an algorithm to improve it may mean fixing problems or simply making it more efficient or maintainable.

Refining code because it does not work correctly

If testing picks up any unexpected results, the algorithm should be inspected and refined to fix any problems.

```
age = input("Enter your age ")
if age >= 18 and age >= 25 then
   print("Young person discount available")
else
   print("No discount available")
endif
```

Test data	Type of test data	Reason	Expected result	Actual result
21	normal	to check valid data accepted and returns expected result	Young person discount available	No discount available
32	normal	to check age > 25 returns 'No discount'	No discount available	Young person discount available

In this case, the inputs 21 and 32 have not produced the expected results.

There is an error in the algorithm in the second line and it needs to be refined:

```
if age >= 18 and age <= 25 then
```

Refining code to make it more efficient or maintainable

+ Code may function but be inefficient or just untidy and difficult to follow.
+ Code that repeats may benefit from being split into subprograms.
+ Repeated code may benefit from being put into an iterative loop.
+ Replacing variable and subprogram names with more meaningful ones will make the code more maintainable.
+ Adding comments to explain how the code works will make it more maintainable.

Check your understanding

4 Describe what is meant by *iterative testing* and why it is important.
5 There are a number of syntax errors in the following program. Identify them and write a corrected version of the program.

```
01 num1 = input("Enter a number ")
02 num1 * 2 = num3
03 num3 = num1 + num2
04 prnit(num3)
```

6 Describe **two** reasons why we might need to refine a program.

Answers on p. 101

Exam checklist

In this chapter you learned about:

Defensive design
+ Defensive design considerations
+ Input validation
+ Maintainability

Testing
+ The purpose of testing
+ Types of testing
+ Identifying syntax and logic errors
+ Selecting and using suitable test data
+ Refining algorithms

1 Describe **three** methods of authenticating a user.
2 List the ways an input might be validated.
3 Describe the features that make code more maintainable.
4 Identify the types of test data that should be used during testing.

Exam-style questions

1 The following code will produce an error.

```
01   x = 100
02   y = 10
03   while y > 0
04       y = y - 1
05       t = x / y
06       print(t)
07   endwhile
```

  a) Identify the error in the program.   [2]
  b) State what kind of error this is.   [1]
  c) Rewrite the code to fix the error.   [2]

2 A program decides if a passenger should be allowed to travel at a reduced rate based on their age.

If the passenger's age is:
+ under 5, then travel is free
+ between 5 and 16 years old, then travel is half price
+ over 16 years, then travel is full price.

Complete the test table below.   [6]

Test data	Type of test data	Expected result
16		half price
− 16		rejected
	erroneous	
		full price

3 A program is designed to decide if a person can use a fairground ride based on their age and height.

To ride the person must be over 10 years old and at least 1.4 metres tall.

```
a = input("Enter a number ")

h = input("Enter a number ")

if a > 10 and h > 1.4 then

print("You may ride")

else

print("Sorry you may not ride")
```

Explain, using examples from this program, **two** ways the maintainability of the program could be improved.   [4]

Answers on p. 106

2.4 Boolean logic

2.4.1 Boolean logic

George Boole was an English mathematician who identified that all logical solutions could be represented using just True and False values. This is the Boolean data type.

Since computers use switches that can be ON or OFF, represented by 1 or 0, these values can be used to represent the True or False values of Boolean logic.

> Boolean data can only be True (1) or False (0).

Simple logic diagrams using the operators AND, OR and NOT

By wiring electronic components together we can create circuits that make simple logical calculations.

We use truth tables to show all the possible input combinations and the resulting output. Inputs are usually labelled with letters from the start of the alphabet, A, B, C, and so on, and outputs with letters from later in the alphabet, P, Q, R, and so on.

NOT gate

The NOT gate simply reverses the input: if we input 1 it outputs 0, if we input 0 it outputs 1.

A	P
0	1
1	0

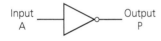

Figure 2.4.1 NOT gate

AND gate

The AND gate outputs 1 only if both inputs are 1, otherwise it outputs 0.

A	B	P
0	0	0
0	1	0
1	0	0
1	1	1

Figure 2.4.2 AND gate

OR gate

The OR gate outputs 1 if either or both of the inputs are 1. If both inputs are 0 it outputs 0.

A	B	P
0	0	0
0	1	1
1	0	1
1	1	1

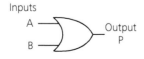

Figure 2.4.3 OR gate

Combining Boolean operators using AND, OR and NOT

We can combine these simple logic gates to form more complex logic circuits:

An AND and a NOT gate:

A	B	R = A AND B	P = NOT R
0	0	0	1
0	1	0	1
1	0	0	1
1	1	1	0

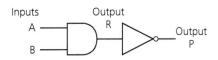

Figure 2.4.4 AND and NOT gate

The output for this circuit can be worked out using a truth table.

Listing all the possible input combinations and identifying the outputs at each stage:

This circuit outputs 1 unless both inputs are 1.

We can describe this circuit using Boolean logic by P = NOT(A AND B)

An AND and an OR gate:

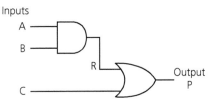

Figure 2.4.5 AND and OR gate

Once again, we build a truth table, but this time we have three inputs, A, B and C giving us eight possible combinations of 1s and 0s for the inputs.

A	B	C	R = A AND B	P = R OR C
0	0	0	0	0
0	0	1	0	1
0	1	0	0	0
0	1	1	0	1
1	0	0	0	0
1	0	1	0	1
1	1	0	1	1
1	1	1	1	1

> **Exam tip**
>
> To make sure you have listed all the possibilities, remember that there should be 2^n rows where n is the number of inputs. For example, with three inputs there are $2^3 = 8$ rows.

This circuit is described in Boolean logic as P = (A AND B) OR C.

> **Exam tip**
>
> It may help you complete the inputs if you notice the pattern of 0s and 1s in each column of inputs from left to right.

Creating logic circuits from expressions

If we are given the Boolean expression to describe a circuit, we can create the truth table and draw the circuit diagram.

P = NOT(A AND B) AND C

Building the truth table gate by gate we get:

A	B	C	A AND B	R = NOT(A AND B)	P = NOT(A AND B) AND C
0	0	0	0	1	0
0	0	1	0	1	1
0	1	0	0	1	0
0	1	1	0	1	1
1	0	0	0	1	0
1	0	1	0	1	1
1	1	0	1	0	0
1	1	1	1	0	0

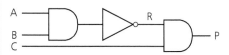

Figure 2.4.6 P = NOT(A AND B) AND C

> **Exam tip**
>
> With Boolean expressions, brackets can be used to specify the order in which operations are applied. In this example, brackets first (A AND B), then NOT then AND.

Applying logical operators in truth tables to solve problems

REVISED

We can use Boolean logic to look at real-life problems creating logical expressions that describe them.

For discounted travel, a company requires that either the traveller be less than 16, or the traveller be over 66 and have a discount travel card.

We can allocate these conditions to:

A is less than 16

B is over 66

C has a discount travel card

Then, we can use these to formulate a Boolean expression.

P = A OR (B AND C)

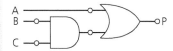

Figure 2.4.7 P = A OR (B AND C)

The truth table is:

A	B	C	R = B AND C	P = A OR (B AND C)
0	0	0	0	0
0	0	1	0	0
0	1	0	0	0
0	1	1	1	1
1	0	0	0	1
1	0	1	0	1
1	1	0	0	1
1	1	1	1	1

> **Exam tip**
>
> When drawing a logic diagram from an expression, use BIDMAS to put the gates in the right order. In this example the brackets tell us to draw B AND C first.

Check your understanding

1 Draw a truth table for the expression P = NOT(A OR B).
2 Draw a truth table for the expression P = (A AND B) OR NOT C.
3 Draw the logic circuit for the expression P = A OR NOT(B AND C).
4 Draw a truth table for this logic circuit and write an expression to describe it.

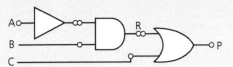

Answers on p. 101

Exam checklist

In this chapter you learned about:

Boolean logic
+ Simple logic diagrams using the operators AND, OR and NOT
+ Truth tables
+ Combining Boolean operators using AND, OR and NOT
+ Applying logical operators in truth tables to solve problems

Now test yourself

TESTED

1 List the **three** main logic gates, draw their diagrams and describe their output.
2 List **all** the possible combinations for **three** inputs.

Exam-style questions

1 State the output from this circuit. [1]

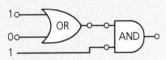

2 Complete the truth table for P = A AND NOT B. [3]

A	B	P= A AND NOT B
0	0	0
0	1	
1	0	
1	1	

3 **a)** Draw the logic circuit for the expression:
P = A OR NOT(B AND C) [3]
b) Complete a truth table for this circuit. [4]

4 Allan wants to buy a second-hand car. He has a maximum of £20 000 to spend. He would like the car to have an electrically heated front windscreen, but if he can buy a hybrid car then this is not a requirement.

Using:

A = costs up to £20 000

B = has an electrically heated front windscreen

C = is a hybrid car

a) Write a Boolean expression, P =, that describes his requirements. [3]
b) Create a truth table for this expression. [4]

Answers on p. 107

2.5 Programming languages and integrated development environments

2.5.1 Languages

In order for the computer to complete any task it needs to be given a suitable set of instructions. These instructions are in the form of programs, but the languages used to provide these instructions can take many forms.

Characteristics and purpose of different levels of programming

There are many languages designed to enable programmers to complete a wide range of tasks, but ultimately the computer can only process instructions in machine code, which is in binary.

Low-level languages

Machine code is a low-level language. This means it can be run directly on the processor.
+ Machine code is dependent on the computer hardware and will not run on different types of computer.
+ Simple instructions, for example to add two numbers, require several machine code instructions to complete – the programmer has to specify each of these individual steps.

Assembly languages replace the use of binary with a mnemonic to represent the instruction, for example replacing the machine code 00100111 with ADD.
+ A program called an **assembler** converts these mnemonics into the binary codes required by the processor before they can be executed.

> Mnemonics are easy to remember codes that represent the machine code operation.

Low-level languages are used when the programmer needs direct access to the hardware to complete a process.
+ One advantage of low-level programs is the high speed that can be achieved through direct access to the hardware.
+ They are used in things such as device drivers or in some embedded systems.

High-level languages

High-level languages use English-like commands that are easier for the programmer to use.
+ Each high-level instruction represents several machine code instructions.
+ High-level languages are not hardware dependent and can be used on different types of computer.
+ High-level languages cannot be run directly by the hardware and must be translated into machine code before they can be run.

Low-level languages	High-level languages
use **binary** (machine code) or mnemonics (assembly language) to represent instructions	use **English-like keywords** such as PRINT and WHILE
hardware dependent – only run on one specific type of computer	**hardware independent** – will run on many different types of computer
refer directly to the computer's hardware; programmers need to understand how the processor works	**abstract** (hide away) the details of the processor. Programmers can concentrate on what the program needs to do
can be **run directly** by the processor	must be **translated into machine code** before they can be run

The purpose of translators

Since computer processors require instructions in machine code, any other language needs to be translated into machine code before it can run.

The characteristics of a compiler and an interpreter

There are two types of translator: compilers and interpreters.

Compilers	Interpreters
translate **every line of code** in a program into machine code and run it afterwards	translate **one line of code** and then run that line, repeating this process for the whole program
produce an executable file	do **not produce** an executable file
program can be **run again without recompiling**; simply run the executable file again	running the program again needs the interpreter to **retranslate every line of code**
executable file can be distributed meaning that users will not see the source code	**no executable file** to distribute; would need to share the source code to distribute the program
compiled code **runs quickly**	because interpreted code has to be translated one command at a time, there is a delay that causes the program to **run more slowly** than compiled code
errors are produced as a long list after compilation; this means it can be difficult to try out ideas since the code needs to be recompiled after every modification	easier to debug code because they translate a line at a time and errors are reported as they occur

> **Exam tip**
>
> It is important to remember that both compilers and interpreters are hardware dependent, even if the language they are translating is the same. A different version of the translator is needed for different hardware.

2.5.2 The integrated development environment (IDE)

An IDE is a software tool providing many of the facilities required to develop a program.

Common tools and facilities available in an IDE

Editor

+ A text editor to allow the programmer to enter or modify code in their chosen language.
+ May include auto-completion of keywords.
+ May include pretty printing to colour code keywords and automatically indent code.

> Pretty printing uses different colours to highlight features of the code to make it easier to spot mistakes.

```
num=int(input('Enter a number '))
for i in range(num,0,-2):
    print(i)
```

Figure 2.5.1 Example of pretty printing from an IDE

Error diagnostics

+ Tools to allow the programmer to find and fix errors.
+ Breakpoints stop the program at a specific point so the programmer can step through the program line by line to investigate how the program runs and help with debugging.
+ Stepping allows the programmer to run the code from this point one line at a time.
+ Variable contents can be checked.

Run-time environment

+ Allows the programmer to run the code from within the IDE.
+ The program output can be seen without opening additional programs.
+ May involve the use of a virtual machine for languages such as Java.
+ May use software that acts as a web server to allow code to run.

> A virtual machine is a software program that behaves like a computer. It makes it possible to run software that the main operating system cannot.

Translators

+ Converts the high-level code into machine code to allow execution by the processor.
+ IDEs include interpreters or compilers (or both).

Check your understanding

1 Explain **one** difference between a high-level language and a low-level language.
2 Explain why programmers use assembly languages.
3 Describe the features that might be found in the error diagnostics of an IDE.
4 Describe the features you might find in the editor of an IDE.

Answers on p. 102

Exam checklist

In this chapter you learned about:

Languages
+ Characteristics and purpose of different levels of programming

+ The purpose of translators
+ The characteristics of a compiler and an interpreter

The integrated development environment (IDE)
+ Common tools and facilities available in an IDE

1   List the advantages of high-level languages over low-level languages.
2   Compare the features of a compiler and an interpreter.
3   List the features typically found in an IDE.

Exam-style questions

1   **a)** Describe what is meant by a *low-level language*.   [2]
    b) Describe the purpose of an assembler.   [2]

2   Abid is using an IDE to develop a program. This IDE includes an editor.
    a) Describe **two** features you might find in an IDE editor.   [4]
    b) Describe **two** other features that might be included in an IDE.   [4]

3   A developer may use an interpreter while developing a program then compile it for distribution.
    a) Explain the advantages of using an interpreter during the development phase.   [4]
    b) Explain why the final program will be compiled for distribution.   [4]

Answers on p. 107

Check your understanding answers

1.1 System architecture

1 The purpose of the CPU is to carry out a set of instructions that is contained in a computer program.

2 **Fetch**: an instruction in the form of data is retrieved from main memory.

Decode: the CPU decodes the binary representation of the instruction

Execute: the CPU performs an action according to the instruction.

3 Any three from:
  + **Accumulator**: stores the results of any calculations made by the Arithmetic Logic Unit.
  + **Program counter**: keeps track of the address of the next instruction.
  + **Memory data register**: stores any data fetched from memory or to be sent to memory.
  + **Memory address register**: stores the location in memory where the MDR needs to fetch data from or send data to.

4 Data and instructions are stored in the same memory.

5 The factors are:
  + Clock speed determines how many fetch–execute cycles can be completed per second.
  + Amount of cache memory determines how much data can be made available for fast transfer to the CPU – accessing cache is much faster than accessing main memory – the more cache the fewer transfers from main memory.
  + The number of cores determines how many processes can be carried out simultaneously. This requires a program to be written to take advantage of multiple cores or for multiple tasks to be run in parallel.

6 Any three from:
  + **Low power** so they can operate effectively from a small power source.
  + **Small in size** so they can fit into a small device.
  + **Rugged** so that they can operate in harsh environments.
  + **Dedicated software** to complete a single task or limited range of tasks such as in a helicopter control system.

1.2 Memory and storage

1 RAM is volatile and data is lost when the power is turned off, therefore it needs ROM to hold the data and instructions to start up the system and RAM to hold the operating system, programs and data it is currently using.

2 Access speeds for secondary storage are slow compared to primary memory.

3 An area of the hard disk used as if it were RAM. It is used to store data from RAM when it needs more memory than available RAM. Data is transferred between RAM and virtual memory as it is required by RAM or no longer immediately required by RAM.

4 The operating system and data and programs so that they are available the next time we switch on the computer.

5 Any three from:
  + **Capacity**: how much data does it need to hold?
  + **Speed**: how quickly can the data be accessed?
  + **Portability**: does the device need to be moved or transported?
  + **Durability**: how robust is the medium?
  + **Reliability**: can it be used over and over again without failing?
  + **Cost**: what is the cost per GB of data stored compared to the requirements?

6 2100 MB

7 $15 \times 6 = 90$ MB

$20 \times 6 = 120$ MB

Total 210 MB

8 a) 11
  b) 51
  c) 76

9 a) 1001010
  b) 10010000
  c) 1010101

10 a) 1010000
  b) 1001001
  c) 1010110

11 a) 5B
  b) AD
  c) F7

12 a) 90
  b) 171
  c) 183

13 a) 1000 1100
  b) 0101 1011
  c) 1111 1110

14 a) A3
  b) CA
  c) 4E

15 a) 100100, 9, 36, multiply by 4
  b) 110, 12, 6, divide by 2
  c) 11100000, 28, 224, multiply by 8
  d) 110, 13, 6, precision lost

16 $2^6 = 64$

17 $32 \times 2000 \times 3000 = 192\,000\,000$ bits

$192\,000\,000 \div 8 = 24\,000\,000$ bytes $= 24\,000$ KB $= 24$ MB

18 The higher the bit depth, the larger the file. The higher the sample rate, the more samples per second, the larger the file size.

19 $22\,000 \times 20 \times 8 = 3\,520\,000$ bits

$3\,520\,000 \div 8 = 440\,000$ bytes $= 440$ MB

20 a) Compression technique that removes data to make the file smaller. The original file cannot be restored.

b) Compression technique that makes the file smaller without losing any data. The original file can be restored.

21 When losing data makes the file unusable; for example, text or programs (or for source copies of images and audio).

1.3 Computer networks, connections and protocols

1 Covers a wide geographical area, computers distributed around several sites, usually includes a connection leased from a telecommunications company.

2 Answers could include:
+ Additional cost of necessary hardware.
+ Malware can spread throughout the network from one infection.
+ Larger systems require staff to manage the system.

3 + Equipment used – individual devices affected by the number of devices sharing the bandwidth.
+ Transmission media – fibre, copper, wireless.

4 Client–server:
+ Request services and resources from a server.
+ Do not store any data.

Peer-to-peer:
+ All computers equal status.
+ All connected to each other.
+ Store and share data with each other.

5 Answers could include:
+ If a server fails then none of the users have access to the service it provides, such as files and software.
+ Server hardware can be very expensive.
+ The whole network can be subject to an attack or malware infection via the server.

6 Reasons could include:
+ Easy to set up.
+ No need for expensive hardware such as a high-end server.
+ Audio streaming to connected speakers.
+ Sharing internet connections.
+ If one device fails, it does not affect the other devices.

7 Answers could include:
+ Does not suffer from interference.
+ Bandwidth of up to 100 Tbps.
+ Distances of 100 km or more.
+ Does not break easily.

8 It uses the MAC address of the device – a unique identifier built into the device.

9 Service set identifier (SSID) is the name of the network broadcast on a wireless network so that clients can identify it and log in.

10 A DNS keeps a record of the IP addresses linked to each website. When a user requests a URL the DNS looks for a matching IP address. If it does not have an address it asks another DNS.

11 Answers could include:
+ Files and applications can be accessed from anywhere providing there is an internet connection.
+ Applications are always up to date.
+ Updates are provided by the cloud providers so there is no need to update individual computers.
+ Storage is flexible and can be upgraded for a price.
+ Backup and security are carried out by the cloud service provider.
+ Data can be shared with others anywhere in the world.

12 Advantages:
+ Robust and reliable since every device has its own connection to the central node.
+ Minimises traffic since data is only directed to the intended node.
+ The failure of one connection does not affect the others.

Disadvantages:
+ Wired star networks require a lot of cabling, which can be intrusive and expensive.
+ If the central switch fails the network fails.

13 Any two from:
+ HTTP
+ HTTPS
+ FTP
+ POP
+ IMAP
+ SMTP

14 Without these standards we would only be able to use hardware and software made by the same manufacturer.

1.4 Network security

1 A Trojan looks like legitimate software, slows the computer and changes settings, and creates backdoors for hackers to access personal information using screenshots and key presses.

2 A form of attack that tricks people into giving away important information or access details.

3 Packet sniffing intercepts data and reads the contents. Wireless networks can be accessed from up to 300 m away from the WAP.

4 A firewall is software or hardware designed to prevent unauthorised access to a network. It inspects incoming and outgoing traffic to ensure that it meets the security criteria in the configured settings.

5 Answers could include:
  + Long passwords that include special characters.
  + Complex passphrases rather than single words.
  + Password manager.
  + Limit the number of login attempts allowed.
  + Two-step authentication.
6 Anti-malware software performs real-time scans of incoming data searching for potential infections and periodic scans of the whole system looking for malicious software.

  Malicious software and infected files are quarantined to prevent them from running and to allow the user to clean or remove them.

1.5 System software

1 Any three from:
  + User interface.
  + Peripheral management.
  + Memory management.
  + File management.
  + User management.
  + Management of data transfers.
  + An interface between the running program and the hardware.
2 The operating system manages any peripheral devices used by the computer. Communication with the peripheral device is controlled by signals produced by the device drivers. Devices drivers are software provided by the manufacturer of the device. Different OSs need different drivers. The driver wakes the device when needed.
3 The OS manages who can access what. It allows users to be created or deleted. It will allocate permission for access to files, folders, applications and settings based on access rights.
4 Encryption scrambles the data so that it cannot be understood if it is accessed by an unauthorised user. It uses keys, or a pair of keys, with an algorithm that scrambles the data; the key is required to unscramble the data.
5 Lossless compression does not remove any detail and the original file can be restored. Lossless compression uses algorithms to look for patterns and repeated elements in a file and stores these in a dictionary with a reference so that the data can be restored.

1.6 Ethical, legal, cultural and environmental impacts of digital technology

1 There are many possible answers, including:
  + Online ordering of more or less anything
  + Logistics systems that control delivery of goods
  + Automated warehouses to pick and ship goods
  + Targeted advertising in, for example, social media
  + Online payment systems
  + Changing work roles from shop based to warehouse based/workstation based.
2 Answers could include:
  + It is useful for finding friends who can be tracked to see where they are/when they will arrive.
  + It can provide valuable evidence for the police to identify where an individual was at the time of an incident/identify who was near an incident.
  + Emergency services can use mobile phone location to identify the scene of an incident in order to attend an emergency.
3 Answers could include:
  + Live facial recognition can be used to identify and locate criminals.
  + Can be used to solve crimes and keep us safe on the streets.
  + Can be used to determine if someone is behaving strangely.
  + Used in airports for fast tracking passengers by comparing facial recognition details stored on the system.
4 The Computer Misuse Act 1990.
5 The data stored should be just that data required for the registered purpose and no more.
6 An organisation that issues licences allowing a user to modify or distribute parts of the software under certain conditions.

2.1 Algorithms

1 Abstraction is removing or hiding unnecessary details from a problem so that the important details can be focused on or more easily understood.
2 Decomposition is breaking a problem down into smaller sub-problems. Once each sub-problem is small and simple enough it can be tackled individually.
3

Line	age	fare	Output	Comment
01	7			
02	7			7 not less than 5 so skip to line 04
04	7			7 is less than 16 so skip
05	7	Half fare		Skip to line 08
08	7	Half fare	Half fare	

4 a) Line 02 `input age`
    Line 09 `if age < 11 then`
  b) Line 06 `if height < 1.5 then`
5 a) C B D A
    C B A D
    B C A D
    B A C D
    A B C D

b)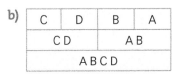

C	D	B	A
C D		A B	
A B C D			

c)

sorted	unsorted
C	D B A
C D	B A
B C D	A
A B C D	

6 A B C D E F G (mid-point = D)

F > D, so discard lower half:

E F G (mid-point = F)

So, item found.

2.2 Programming fundamentals

1 a) x = 3
   b) x = 10
   c) x = 5
   d) x = 3
   e) x = 4
2 a) False
   b) True
   c) True
   d) True
   e) True
3 a) string
   b) integer
   c) Boolean
   d) real
   e) string
   f) character
   g) string
4 a) 8
   b) evi
   c) FRANK
   d) Frank's revision
5 a) Cohen, Holland, Hernandez
   b) Birmingham, 3

   London, 7
   c) Amaya
6 a) 'Poppy'
   b) plant[0,2]

2.3 Producing robust programs

1 Two-factor authentication uses electronic devices to send a code, or request additional actions, to authenticate a user who has logged in using a username and password.
2 Gender must be one of two values, male or female.

Wingspan should be within a reasonable range of values/must be a real number/must be a numeric value.

3 Features could include:
   + Commenting to explain what each bit does.
   + Meaningful variable names to describe the data that the variable contains.
   + Indentation to show where loops start and end.
   + Modular program/use of subprograms to structure repeated code effectively.
4 Iterative testing is testing during development at a modular level to check the individual parts of the program work as expected. As each new module is added the program is tested to check that no new errors have been introduced and that data from previous modules works with the new one. Identifying faults in an individual module may be harder once modules are combined.
5 02 num1 * 2 = num3 should be num3 = num1 * 2

03 num2 has not been defined

04 prnit is incorrect spelled; it should be print
6 Any two from:
   + Code may be inefficient.
   + Repeated code may be put into subprograms/ loops.
   + The requirements of the program may have changed since it was first developed.
   + Errors may have been identified since it was first released.
   + Making the code more maintainable with meaningful descriptive names and/or adding comments to explain the code.

2.4 Boolean logic

1

A	B	A OR B	NOT(A OR B)
0	0	0	1
0	1	1	0
1	0	1	0
1	1	1	0

2

A	B	C	A AND B	(A AND B) OR NOTC
0	0	0	0	1
0	0	1	0	0
0	1	0	0	1
0	1	1	0	0
1	0	0	0	1
1	0	1	0	0
1	1	0	1	1
1	1	1	1	1

3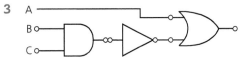

4

A	B	C	NOTA AND B	(NOTA AND B) OR C
0	0	0	0	0
0	0	1	0	1
0	1	0	1	1
0	1	1	1	1
1	0	0	0	0
1	0	1	0	1
1	1	0	0	0
1	1	1	0	1

An expression which describes this is:
(NOTA AND B) OR C

2.5 Programming languages and integrated development environments

1 Differences could include:
   + Low-level languages use binary (machine code) or mnemonics (assembly language) to represent instructions while high-level languages use English-like keywords such as PRINT and WHILE.
   + Low-level languages are hardware dependent (only run on one specific type of computer) while high-level languages are hardware independent (will run on many different types of computer).

   + Low-level languages refer directly to the computer's hardware. Programmers need to understand how the processor works. High-level languages abstract (hide away) the details of the processor. Programmers can concentrate on what the program needs to do.
   + Low-level languages can be run directly by the processor while high-level languages must be translated into machine code before they can be run.

2 + Assembly languages have all the advantages of low-level programming such as high speed of execution through direct access to hardware.
   + Use mnemonics that indicate what the command does rather than binary so easier to use.

3 + Breakpoints to stop the program at a specific point so the programmer can step through the program line by line to investigate how the program run and help with debugging.
   + Stepping allows the programmer to run the code from this point one line at a time.
   + The contents of variables can be checked.

4 Features include:
   + A text editor to allow the programmer to enter or modify code in their chosen language.
   + Auto-completion of keywords.
   + Pretty printing to colour code keywords and automatically indent code.

Exam-style question answers

1.1 System architecture

1 a) Clock speed determines the processor speed, the higher the speed the more instructions can be fetched and executed per second [1] and the faster a program will run [1].

b) Any two from:
+ Cache is located between RAM and CPU providing fast access to data [1].
+ Data is moved into cache ready to be used by the CPU [1].
+ If there is more cache more data can be ready for the CPU when it is required [1].

c) Stores the memory location [1] for data to be fetched from or sent to [1].

d) If a program is written to take advantage of multiple cores [1] the CPU can process more than one fetch–execute cycle simultaneously [1].

2 a) Washing programs/control program for water temperature or level, and so on [1].

b) Any two from selected program [1], wash temperature [1], spin speed [1], *other sensible example* [1].

c) Rugged [1] to withstand working in a harsh environment within a car engine [1]; Small [1] to fit into a small device mounted within the car engine [1]; Dedicated function [1] designed to do just one task, control the engine [1].

[1 mark for the feature, one for the explanation, maximum of 4 marks]

3 a) Arithmetic operations [1] such as add, subtract [1]; Logical operations [1] such as AND, NOT, OR [1]; Binary shifts [1] shifting the binary values multiplies or divides the number [1].

b) The address of the next instruction is copied from the program counter and placed in the MAR [1]; The control unit fetches the data that is stored at that address and copies it to the MDR [1]; The program counter is incremented to point to the next instruction [1].

1.2 Memory and storage

1 a) 1000101 [1]

b) 6C [1]

c)

		1	1	0	1	0	1
+		1	0	0	1	1	1
	1	0	1	1	1	0	0
		1		1	1	1	

[1 mark for LH nibble (0)111; 1 mark for RH nibble 1100; 1 mark for working]

d) i) 39 [1]

ii) 1001110 – 78 [1]

iii) 10011 – 19 [1] loss of accuracy (since 39 ÷ 2 = 19.5) [1]

2 a) The number of bits used to store each sampled value [1].

b) The more bits we use, the more accurately we can represent the data for that sample point [1], providing a better representation of the original sound [1].

c) $41\,000 \times 15 \times 16$ [1]

$= 9\,840\,000$ [1]

$9\,840\,000 \div 8 = 1\,230\,000$ bytes [1]

$= 1.23$ MB [1]

3 a) The number of bits used per pixel [1].

b) The number of pixels per unit of distance – dots per inch (DPI) [1].

c) The more bits per pixel, the larger the range of colours we can have in the image [1].

The more colours we have available, the better the representation of the image [1].

The more pixels we use per inch, the greater the detail stored [1].

This enables us to enlarge the image more and reduce the amount of pixelation. [1].

d) [1 mark each for the reason and explanation, maximum 2 marks]:
+ In images there are large blocks of very similar colours that can be combined [1] without significantly affecting the quality of the image [1].
+ If the number of colours used is reduced [1] we may not be able to tell the difference [1 (and it may not significantly affect the image).

4 It is a list of all the characters available to the computer [1]. It includes all the standard characters and any extra symbols, such as windings, emoji, and so on [1].

1.3 Computer networks, connections and protocols

1 a) Any two from: Share resources/devices [1]; Share data [1]; Communication between users [1].

b) Any two from: Easy to set up [1]; No expensive or intrusive wiring required [1]; Easy to add new devices [1]; The location of devices is not fixed by wired connection points [1].

c) Any two from: Can share information between branches [1]; Communication between users/branches [1]; Details of properties stored at each branch can be available in all branches [1] without needing to duplicate data [1].

My Revision Notes: OCR GCSE Computer Science

d) The router will connect the LANs in each branch together [1] using a leased line from a telecommunications company/via the internet [1].

2 a) Any two from: All the devices are connected directly or indirectly to each other [1]; There is no central switch [1]; Computers store their own data [1] and also pass on data from other devices [1].

b) Reliable/robust, no single point of failure [1]; In the event of a fault there are multiple communications routes [1]; Multiple routes means the network can handle high volumes of traffic [1].

3 a) Every device connected to a network is assigned an IP address when it connects [1]. This address is used to locate the device on the network [1].

b) When a user requests a URL the DNS looks for a matching IP address [1]. If it does not have an address it asks another DNS [1]. This process continues until the IP is found or an error message is returned [1].

4 a) Software applications [1]; Data storage [1].

b) [1 mark each, maximum 6 marks]:
+ Files and applications can be accessed from anywhere providing there is an internet connection [1].
+ Data can be shared with others anywhere in the world [1].
+ Applications are always up to date [1].
+ Updates are provided by the cloud providers so there is no need to update individual computers [1].
+ No need to update storage facilities [1].
+ Storage is flexible and can be upgraded (for a price) [1].
+ No need to keep backups or provide backup facilities [1].
+ Backup and security are carried out by the cloud service provider [1].

5 When data is sent by a client the individual packets of data are wrapped in information to ensure the packet is transmitted successfully [1]. Protocols or rules are assigned to layers [1] so that the data passes through each layer in turn to prepare it for transmission and the necessary information is added [1]. When data is received it passes through these layers in reverse order to recover the data, removing the additional information used to transmit it [1].

1.4 Network security

1 [1 mark each for the reason and explanation, maximum 6 marks]:
+ Strong wireless password [1] to make the network hard to hack into [1].
+ Encryption of data and files [1] so that if accessed they are unreadable without the key [1].

+ MAC address authentication [1] so that only known devices can access the network [1].
+ Anti-malware software [1] will reduce the risk of malware being installed that can provide information to a hacker to enable access to the network [1].

2 a) SQL injection can bypass security by inputting valid SQL expressions instead of user details [1]. This causes a sequence of commands to be executed resulting in the release of sensitive data [1].

b) [1 mark each for the reason and explanation, maximum 2 marks]:
+ Use input validation [1] to set password and username rules that do not permit characters which can be used in SQL injection attacks [1].
+ Use input sanitisation [1] to remove special characters and SQL command words from an input before processing it [1].

3 a) Any two from:
Testers use hacking techniques [1] to attempt to break into a system to identify vulnerabilities that can be exploited in an attack [1]. They will also assess the ability of the organisation to respond to an attack and to recover any data that is lost or compromised [1].

b) i) A set of rules that all users of networks should follow [1] and procedures for managing the network [1].

ii) [1 mark for each named item, maximum 3 marks, plus 1 mark for each description/example, maximum 3 marks]:
+ Password requirements [1]: rules about length of password, use of symbols, regular changes [1].
+ The use of removable devices [1]: no access to USB or optical drives [1].
+ An acceptable use policy [1]: rules about the use of email and the web [1].
+ The type and frequency of backup [1]: for example, full or incremental backups scheduled [1].
+ Security measures to be used [1]: for example, off-site backup storage, firewall rules [1].
+ User access rights [1]: user groups with appropriate access rights, who has access to what [1].

1.5 System software

1 a) i) A GUI is a Graphical User interface [1] where the user interacts with the computer hardware through software that provides graphics to represent operations; these can be activated using an input device such as a touchscreen or mouse. [1].

ii) [1 mark for feature, 1 mark for description, maximum 4 marks]:
+ **Windows** [1] to run applications or display the contents of a folder [1].
+ **Icons** [1] to represent applications or utilities [1].
+ **Menus** [1] to offer options or features [1].
+ **Pointer** [1] that can be moved to a location on screen to select items or perform actions [1].

b) [maximum 2 marks]:
+ Andrew will allocate access rights to files and applications [1] so his son cannot access his personal files [1].
  OR
+ Access to specific applications will be controlled [1]; can control access to the internet OR prevent accessing unsuitable sites [1].

c) i) Images are large files so compressed files can be transmitted much more quickly over the internet [1]. When emailing files there is often a limit on the size of an attachment so large files need to be compressed [1].
   ii) Lossy [1] because we can only see a limited range of colours, so images do not suffer from the removal of colours by reducing the colour depth (removing some colours) OR large blocks of similar colours can be merged without any significant loss to the image [1].

2 a) File management is a feature of the OS responsible for storing and retrieving files [1] to and from secondary storage [1].

b) [1 mark for feature, 1 mark for description, maximum 4 marks]:
+ Provides facilities to manage files [1], such as save, delete, move, and so on. [1]
+ Manages the secondary storage [1] dividing it up into identifiable areas so that the location of each file can be stored in an index [1].
+ Creates file structures [1] so that it is easier for the user to organise and locate files [1].
+ Determines what to do with a file based on its type [1], such as execute a file or open a suitable application [1].

c) [1 mark for identification, 1 mark for description, maximum 4 marks]:
+ **Encryption** [1]: scrambles the data so that it cannot be understood if it is accessed by an unauthorised user [1].
+ **Defragmentation** [1]: organises and moves the separate parts of the data files so that they are stored together and can be accessed much more quickly [1].
+ **Data compression** [1]: uses algorithms to reduce the size of a file [1].

3 a) A collection of programs that are used in most computer devices to tell the hardware what to do [1] and allow the user to interact with the device [1].

b) [1 mark for identification, 1 mark for description, maximum 6 marks]:
+ A user interface [1] to allow the user to interact with the system [1].
+ An interface [1] between the running program and the hardware [1].
+ Peripheral management [1] to control devices using driver software [1].
+ Memory management [1] to allocate memory to running programs [1].
+ Management of data transfers [1] between memory locations, the CPU and secondary storage [1].
+ File management [1] to allow users to organise their work into folders [1].
+ User management [1] to control access to the system, files and software [1].

1.6 Ethical, legal, cultural and environmental impacts of digital technology

1 a) Discussion could include any of the following [maximum 4 marks]:
+ Available skill set to manage and maintain the software [1] given no support from the creator [1].
+ Cost advantage with open source [1].
+ Can use on several machines [1].
+ Availability of community support [1].
+ Interaction with other software used in the business [1] or with software used by suppliers/customers [1].

b) Discussion could include any of the following [maximum 4 marks]:
+ Access to unsuitable sites [1], comments made by employees reflecting badly on the business [1].
+ Employees spending excessive time on the internet [1] and not doing their job [1].
+ Access to illegal sites [1] and the employer's responsibility for illegal acts [1].
+ Illegal behaviour by the employee (such as trolling or bullying) [1] reflects badly on the employer [1].

2 Discussion question:

0 marks: No response or response does not cover any related issues

1–2 marks: One or two points identified without comment and not clearly related to the scenario

3–5 marks: Points made relate to the scenario with some detailed discussion but may be one-sided

6–8 marks: A balanced discussion of the issues using a range of relevant points each discussed in suitable detail.

Points may cover:
+ Use of electricity by data centres.
+ Use of rare substances within the technology, depleting resources.

- Energy used to manufacture devices.
- Toxic materials used and their disposal.

Benefits to the environment might include:

- Reduced use of paper and physical documents.
- Reduced environmental damage from travel, because of virtual meetings.

2.1 Algorithms

1

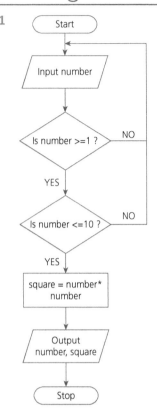

[1 mark for input, 1 mark for each decision (or 2 marks for decision with correct logical combination), 1 mark for process, 1 mark for output, 1 mark for correct flow, maximum 6 marks]

2
```
total = 0
for index = 1 to 5
    num = input("Enter a new number ")
    total = total + num
next index
avg = total/5
print(avg)
```
[1 mark for initialising a variable for total; 1 mark for for loop 1 to 5; 1 mark for input; 1 mark for adding input value to the total; 1 mark for calculating the average (this may be done as part of the print statement); 1 mark for outputting the average, maximum 6 marks]

3 a)

ivy	broom	poppy	fern	privet	lilac	dogwood	rose	[1]

broom, ivy	fern, poppy	lilac, privet	dogwood, rose	[1]

broom, fern, ivy, poppy	dogwood, lilac, privet, rose	[1]

broom, dogwood, fern, ivy, lilac, poppy, privet, rose	[1]

b) A merge sort creates a list for every item in the original list and each combined list [1] taking up large amounts of memory [1].

4 a) cat, dog, frog, goat, horse, kangaroo, lion, monkey, parrot
   mid-point = horse; lion > horse [1]
   so delete lower half [1]
   kangaroo, lion, monkey, parrot
   mid-point = lion (choose left-hand side of middle values); lion, so item found [1]
   b) Seven steps required [1].
   c) Binary search requires the list to be in order [1] so a linear search required if the list is not sorted [1].

2.2 Programming fundamentals

1 A variable is a memory location (with an identifier) [1] storing a value that can change [1]. Unlike a variable, the value stored in a constant cannot be changed while the program is running [1].

2 0 0 [1]
   1 3 [1]
   2 6 [1]

3
```
total = 0
for index = 0 to 4
    total = total + value[index]
print(total)
```
[1 mark for initialisation, 1 mark for for loop, 1 mark for correct range, 1 mark for adding to total, 1 mark for correct array index, 1 mark for outputting the result]

4 a) London [1]
   Oslo [1]
   b) 15, 22 [1]
   23, 19 [1]
   c) `SELECT *` [1]
   `FROM tblCities` [1]
   `WHERE rainfall < 10` [1]

2.3 Producing robust programs

1 a) y can take the value 0 [1] producing division by zero in line 05 [1]
   b) Logic error [1]
   c) [two possibilities to fix the problem; either scores 2 marks]
   Swap lines 04 and 05
   Change line 03 to `while y > 1`

2 Example answers in bold; these or similar values are required [1 mark per correct item].

Test data	Type of test data	Expected result
16	**boundary**	half price
16	**invalid**	rejected
[any non-numeric value for example]	erroneous	**rejected**
18 [any value over 16]	**normal**	full price

3 [1 mark for each reason, 1 mark for each explanation, maximum 4 marks]:
- Meaningful variable names [1] such as `age` instead of `a` and `height` instead of `h` [1].
- Indent code [1] between `if` and `else` [1].
- Meaningful prompts [1]; instead of "`Enter a number`", use "`Enter age`" and "`Enter height`" [1].

2.4 Boolean logic

1 1 [1]

2

A	B	P= A AND NOT B	
0	0	0	
0	1	**0**	[1]
1	0	**1**	[1]
1	1	**0**	[1]

3 a)

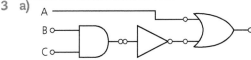

[1 mark for B AND C, 1 mark for NOT in the right place after (B AND C), 1 mark A OR NOT (B and C)]

b)

A	B	C	NOT(B AND C)	A OR NOT(B AND C)
0	0	0	1	1
0	0	1	1	1
0	1	0	1	1
0	1	1	0	0
1	0	0	1	1
1	0	1	1	1
1	1	0	1	1
1	1	1	0	1

[1 mark for correct ABC columns; 1 mark for B AND C; 1 mark for NOT(B AND C) – may be combined; 1 mark for final column]

4 a) A AND (B OR C)

[1 mark for AND; 1 mark for B OR C; 1 mark for correct use of brackets]

b)

A	B	C	B OR C	A AND (B OR C)
0	0	0	0	0
0	0	1	1	0
0	1	0	1	0
0	1	1	1	0
1	0	0	0	0
1	0	1	1	1
1	1	0	1	1
1	1	1	1	1

[1 mark for correct ABC columns; 1 mark for B OR C; 1 mark for first four rows of final column; 1 mark for last four rows of final column]

2.5 Programming languages and integrated development environments

1 a) Any two from:
- Low-level languages run directly on the hardware [1].
- One instruction per fetch–execute cycle [1].
- Hardware dependent/cannot run on different hardware [1].

b) An assembler is used to convert assembly language programs into machine code OR direct one-to-one relationship with machine code [1]. It uses mnemonics to represent machine code instructions to make it easier for the programmer to understand the instructions [1].

2 a) [1 mark for each reason, 1 mark for each explanation, maximum 4 marks]:
- A text editor [1] to allow the programmer to enter or modify code in their chosen language [1].
- Auto-completion of keywords [1] to reduce possible typos [1].
- Pretty printing [1] to colour code keywords and automatically indent code [1].

b) [1 mark for each feature, 1 mark for each explanation, maximum 4 marks]:
- Error diagnostics [1] to allow the programmer to find and fix errors [1].
- Run-time environment [1] to run the code from within the IDE [1].
- Translators [1] to convert the high-level code into machine code to allow execution by the processor [1].

3 a) Easier to debug code [1] because it translates a line at a time and errors are reported as they occur [1]. Translating one line at a time also means the developer can create the code in small segments [1] to try out ideas [1].

b) The compiled code is virtually unreadable so it is difficult for a user to modify the code [1]; this provides some protection for intellectual property [1]. The code can be run on the target environment directly without the end user needing a suitable translator [1]. The code will run much more quickly since it does not need to be translated [1].

INDEX